Building Bright Minds

Building *Bright* Minds

SARAH J. FOSTER

A *Gentle Parenting Guide* for Raising *Mentally Strong* and *Emotionally Healthy* Kids

Disclaimer Notice

The information and exercises in this book, are intended for educational and informational purposes only. They are not a substitute for professional guidance from a qualified parenting expert or child development specialist.

If your child exhibits concerning behaviors or struggles significantly, please seek consultation with a licensed therapist or other qualified professional. While the author strives to provide accurate and up-to-date information, child development is a constantly evolving field. It's always best to seek personalized advice from a qualified professional regarding your child's specific needs and circumstances.

The techniques and strategies in this book have the potential to be helpful, but results are not guaranteed. The author and publisher are not responsible for any outcomes resulting from the use or misuse of the information provided. As a parent, you are ultimately responsible for your choices, actions, and the results you experience in raising your child.

Copyright Notice

Kindread Publishing
367 St Marks Ave Brooklyn, NY
11238
https://www.kindread.org

Building Bright Minds
Copyright © 2024 by Sarah J. Foster

For more information, email info@kindread.org

First Edition

ISBN: 9798891701205

To Mom, the first gentle guide who taught me the importance of fostering curiosity and resilience in children.

Preface

Welcome aboard the parenthood rollercoaster! It's a thrilling ride filled with breathtaking wonder and moments that bewilders you. One minute you're building a masterpiece of blocks, the next you're facing a meltdown that rivals a rock concert. But that's the endearing (and sometimes chaotic) beauty of it all!

Think of this book as your warm and supportive partner on this incredible adventure. We'll delve into practical tools to navigate those inevitable tantrums, celebrate your child's insatiable curiosity, and most importantly, build an unbreakable bond with your little one.

Here, judgment and rigid rules are left at the door. Instead, we'll explore real-life scenarios, share engaging activities that spark joy and offer prompts for self-reflection so you can grow alongside your child. Remember, you're never alone in this!

Let's be honest, parenting is messy. Some days, those brilliant minds might seem more like "bright chaos." But that's perfectly okay! This book is here to celebrate the laughter, acknowledge the challenges, and equip you with gentle tools to nurture your child's potential. Every giggle, every cuddle, every learning adventure—it all adds up to something extraordinary.

Here's to your incredible journey together and the amazing little minds you're helping to flourish!

With encouragement and warmth,

Sarah J. Foster

How To Use This Book

Think of this book as your trusty sidekick on the wild and wonderful journey of parenting, or caregiving! We've organized it to follow your child's development, from those precious early days to the exciting leaps of toddlerhood and beyond. But here's the secret: even though chapters are tailored to specific ages, every single page is brimming with wisdom that can be applied at any stage and by any caregiver.

Whether you're a parent, grandparent, aunt, uncle, foster parent, adoptive parent, or any other loving adult playing a significant role in a child's life, this book is for you. We understand that the titles we hold may differ, but the love and commitment we share for these little ones is boundless. So, go ahead, dive in from cover to cover, and soak it all in!

As your child grows and changes (sometimes faster than you can refill the snack drawer!), feel free to revisit sections that feel most relevant to your current stage. For example, if your little one is now a bustling toddler, you might find yourself drawn to the chapters on navigating tantrums and encouraging independence. Later on, you might circle back to sections on fostering friendships or supporting emotional development. This book isn't meant to be read just once and then forgotten. It's a resource you can return to again and again, finding new insights and inspiration each time, as your child reaches new milestones and faces new challenges.

Remember, every child is unique, and there's no one-size-fits-all approach. Trust your instincts, adapt the suggestions to fit your family, and most importantly, give yourself grace. We're all learning and growing together, caregivers and children alike.

Contents

Introduction

Have you ever felt overwhelmed by the amount of parenting advice? Sifting through endless articles and conflicting recommendations can leave you feeling lost, wondering what truly matters when it comes to raising your child.

Here's the truth: parenting is both the most challenging and the most rewarding experience of life. Yes, there will be sleepless nights and frustrating moments. But there will also be countless opportunities to witness your child's wonder as they discover the world around them and to revel in the deep, unconditional love that comes with parenthood.

Imagine parenting not just as a demanding job, but as a beautiful journey of mutual growth. You guide your child as they explore the world, revealing its wonders and their own hidden potential. In turn, this journey unveils your own strengths and capabilities as a parent.

The world your child experiences can be as exciting as it is confusing. They lack the understanding and tools to navigate its complexities and challenges effectively. That's where you come in – your support is essential in building the foundation for their "bright mind" and nurturing the resilience that will help them thrive.

This book is your compass, your guide, and your source of inspiration as you embark on this extraordinary adventure. Together, we'll explore how to raise a child who is not only intelligent but also emotionally strong, confident, and resilient – a child who is equipped to face life's challenges with grace and determination.

But how do you navigate this remarkable journey? To help your child thrive, you need a roadmap. This roadmap includes understanding your child's developmental needs at each stage, navigating their emotions, creating a strong bond, and continuously expanding your parenting knowledge.

This book is precisely that roadmap. We'll explore the unique challenges and joys of each stage, from the wonder-filled world of infants to the independent spirit of teenagers. Each chapter delves into the commonalities within these age groups, helping you understand the core needs of your child at each point in their development:

- **The Miracle of Life: Pregnancy and Preparing for Parenthood:** The journey of parenthood begins long before your baby arrives. This stage is filled with anticipation, excitement, and a cascade of emotions. As you prepare for the arrival of your little one, you'll learn how to create a nurturing environment for both yourself and your baby, laying the foundation for a strong and healthy start.

- **The Enchanted World of Babies (Infants):** Imagine a world where everything is new and fascinating. This is your baby's world. The first year is a whimsical dance of rapid development, from cooing and gurgling to rolling and crawling. Your role is to create a safe and loving environment that promotes exploration and communication. By responding to their cues and building a strong bond, you lay the groundwork for emotional well-being and a lifelong love of learning.

- **The Curious Climber: The Toddler Years:** Toddlers are all about exploration and independence. They're determined to conquer their world, one wobbly step at a time. This stage is also marked by a surge in emotions, which can sometimes lead to tantrums and meltdowns. Your guidance and patience are crucial in helping your toddler navigate these big feelings. Through gentle discipline and positive reinforcement, you can set boundaries while nurturing their natural curiosity.

- **The Knowledge Seekers:** Elementary School: The elementary years are a time of remarkable intellectual growth. Your child will blossom into a little scholar, eager to learn about math, science, history, and the world around them. This stage also sees the development of social skills as children interact with friends and classmates. Your role is to nurture their curiosity, provide a supportive learning environment, and guide them in navigating the social complexities of childhood.

- **Navigating the Wild Ride:** Teenagers: Teenage years are often described as a rollercoaster for a reason. This period is marked by rapid physical and emotional changes, along with a growing desire for independence. Teenagers are grappling with their identity, forming close friendships, and exploring romantic relationships. Your role is to be a supportive guide, offering clear boundaries while fostering open communication and trust. By creating a safe space for your teenager to express themselves, you can help them navigate this challenging yet exciting stage.

This journey of gentle parenting doesn't end once your child reaches adulthood. The bond you forge will last a lifetime, even as they grow and create their own families. Let's embark on this incredible adventure together.

66

Childhood is not a race to be won, but a journey to be savored.

- GRAYCE ARRINGTON

(An American author and motivational speaker)

Part 1:

Embracing the Adventure: Preparing for Your Little Wonder

Inside This Part

As soon as-to-be parents, you're about to embark on the incredible adventure of parenthood. It's a beautiful blend of feelings – a mix of excitement, wonder, and maybe even a touch of nervousness. But fear not, you're not alone in this journey!

This part of the book is designed to be your warm and supportive companion as you prepare to welcome your "little wonder" into the world. Here, we'll delve into the fascinating world of prenatal development, learning how your baby's tiny body and amazing abilities are building even before they take their first breath. We'll explore how to create a healthy environment for your growing baby, nurturing their physical well-being and laying the foundation for a healthy future.

Most importantly, we'll focus on building that all-important bond with your little one, right from the start. This deep connection, fostered by both parents, is the foundation for a happy, secure child. We'll share heartfelt tips and tricks to nurture this bond throughout pregnancy, ensuring that both you and your partner feel deeply connected to your growing baby.

Finally, we'll equip you with your own "emotional toolkit," helping you navigate the rollercoaster of emotions that comes with parenthood. By understanding your own emotional responses, you'll be better prepared to create a calm and loving environment for both you and your baby. So buckle up, grab this book together, and let's embark on this incredible journey as a team!

The Miracle of Prenatal Development: *Understanding Your Baby's Early Development*

The incredible moment you discover you're expecting — a tiny universe ignites within, setting the stage for a spectacular journey that will shape your child's entire life.

Even before you see that first flutter on the ultrasound, your baby's incredible growth kicks off. Millions of tiny cells are multiplying, forming the foundation for their whole body and amazing abilities. It's like a miniature light show, with connections sparking and solidifying at an astonishing rate.

As the weeks tick by, this miraculous process continues. Sensory pathways develop, allowing your baby to experience the world around them in a muffled way. They might hear a parent's heartbeat, the rumble of a caregiver's voice, or even the comforting melodies you play together. It's a sensory soup, a prelude to the explosion of sights, sounds, and smells that await them once they arrive.

The Miracle of Connection Starts Early

The miracle of prenatal development goes far beyond physical growth. It's a time when the connection between you and your baby begins to blossom. While you might think this bond starts when you first hold your little one, the reality is even more amazing. Even before birth, your baby can experience the world around them through muffled sounds and sensations. They might even pick up your emotions! This incredible process highlights the powerful connection that exists from the start. It's more than just waiting for your baby to arrive — it's about nurturing a loving bond right from the start.

This early stage is also crucial for emotional development. Believe it or not, studies suggest babies can begin to experience basic emotions even before birth. They might react to stress hormones in a caregiver's body, feeling a sense of calm or anxiety depending on the situation. It's a powerful reminder of the deep connection between you, the expecting parents, and your little one, even before they take their first breath.

Now, this might sound overwhelming with all this complex development happening inside one of you. But here's the amazing thing: you, as soon-to-be parents, play a vital role in this incredible process! By taking care of yourselves, both physically and emotionally, you're taking care of your baby's growing foundation.

Partnering Up: How Dads Can Help During This Period

Pregnancy is an incredible journey, filled with a rollercoaster of emotions for both parents. While the expecting parent experiences the physical changes of carrying a new life, the other parent has a vital role to play in offering unwavering support and fostering a strong bond with both the expecting parent and the baby.

Imagine attending prenatal appointments together, holding hands as you witness the first grainy ultrasound image of your tiny miracle. Asking questions and learning about your baby's development side-by-side will make you feel informed and empowered as a team. Reading books and articles about pregnancy together can be a great way to ease anxieties and prepare for parenthood. Discussing your hopes and dreams for this little one strengthens your bond and creates a sense of shared purpose.

Pregnancy can be physically demanding, and the other parent can be a superhero in disguise! Helping with household chores, running errands, or offering a gentle massage can alleviate stress and allow the expecting parent time to rest and focus on self-care. Remember, a little goes a long way. A warm bath drawn, a healthy meal prepared, or simply offering a listening ear can make a world of difference.

Emotional support is as important as physical support. Be a safe space for the expecting parent, offering words of encouragement and validating their feelings, whether they're experiencing excitement, anxiety, or anything in between. This rollercoaster of emotions is normal, and simply being present and understanding can be incredibly comforting.

Even before their much-anticipated arrival, the expecting parent's partner can play a key role in building a bond with the baby. Gently placing a hand on the pregnant parent's belly and talking to the little one creates a connection. Playing calming music or reading aloud creates a peaceful and stimulating environment for the baby to develop and hear their voices.

By actively participating in these ways, both parents can provide invaluable support throughout pregnancy. It's a team effort, and fostering a strong connection with both the expecting parent and the baby lays the foundation for a happy and healthy family life.

Creating a Thriving Environment for Your Little One is Next

You've both been there every step of the way, supporting each other and witnessing the incredible development of your tiny miracle. Now, with the excitement of your baby's arrival on the horizon, you might be wondering: "How can we create the best possible environment for this little adventurer to thrive?"

The good news is that you, as parents-to-be, can build a fantastic nest for your baby, even before their arrival. Think of it as a team effort – you've been there for each other throughout pregnancy, and now you can continue that strong bond as you prepare for parenthood together.

In the upcoming sections, we'll explore practical tips that go beyond cute crib sheets (although those are important too!). We'll talk about creating a safe and stimulating space for your little one, making healthy lifestyle choices that benefit everyone in the family, and even some fun ways to connect as a family before they arrive. So, grab your partner, because this next step is all about creating a loving foundation for your bright little mind. We'll be your guide, cheering you on as you build a world that fosters curiosity, confidence, and resilience – the cornerstones of a happy and healthy childhood. Let's do this!

In Action: Finding Calm in the Chaos

✓ **Emily's Serenity:** Balancing a demanding career with a surprise pregnancy left Emily stressed. Worried about the impact on her baby, she embraced a newfound tool: meditation. Starting with just five minutes a day, Emily focused on calming her breath and connecting with the tiny life within her. Gradually, the constant tension eased, replaced by a sense of peace. This newfound calm wasn't just for her – it created a more relaxed atmosphere at home, benefiting both mom and baby.

✓ **David Dives In:** Drowning in prenatal advice, David felt overwhelmed. Partner's friend, a seasoned mom, mentioned creating a stimulating environment for the baby. A spark ignited! David didn't need to be an expert. He started with simple acts of love: nightly readings and calming music. These small steps empowered him and built a bond with his unborn child.

Thriving Together:
Building a Healthy Foundation for Baby and Parents

Congratulations! You've officially entered the nesting phase of parenthood. It's a time of bubbling excitement, eager anticipation, and maybe even a touch of nesting frenzy. But fear not, new parents! This doesn't have to be all about paint colors and crib sheets (although picking those out can be fun too!). We're here to guide you on creating a safe, stimulating, and nurturing environment for your little miracle, even before they arrive.

Imagine building a cozy haven for your tiny adventurer. Forget about creating a picture-perfect nursery straight out of a magazine (though, hey, if that's your thing, go for it!). This is more about establishing a foundation that fosters your baby's development and strengthens the bond between you, your partner, and your soon-to-arrive family member.

Safety First: A Secure Haven for Your Little One

Safety first! Before your little explorer arrives, it's important to create a safe haven. Don't worry, you're not alone in wanting to make everything perfect for your baby. It's natural to feel a surge of protectiveness, and a little detective work goes a long way. Imagine crawling around on the floor — that's your baby's perspective! What could they potentially grab, climb on, or put in nature?

Those tiny fingers and toes will be on the move faster than you think. They'll go from curious observers to little adventurers in a blink, so it's best to baby-proof with this early exploration in mind. Before your curious crawler becomes a determined climber, take some proactive measures to create a safe haven for your precious arrival.

Securing Your Space:

- Anchor furniture to walls using sturdy anchors to prevent toppling over during enthusiastic climbing attempts.
- Install childproof locks on all cabinets, especially those containing cleaning supplies, medications, or sharp objects.
- Consider adding soft corner protectors to tables, coffee tables, and other furniture with sharp edges to prevent bumps.

Electrical Safety and Beyond:

- Ensure you've installed tamper-resistant outlet covers throughout the house to prevent electrical accidents.
- Minimize clutter on floors that could cause slips and falls. Consider using non-slip mats in high-traffic areas like bathrooms and kitchens.
- Assemble a basic first-aid kit with bandages, antiseptic wipes, and a thermometer to be prepared for minor bumps and scrapes.

By taking these steps now, you can create a safe and stimulating environment that allows your little one to confidently explore their world from the get-go.

Creating a Cozy Crib: Your Baby's Sleep Sanctuary

Sleep is essential for your little one's development, so their crib needs to be a haven of comfort and safety. Keep it clutter-free – a firm mattress with a breathable, lightweight blanket is all they truly need. Resist the urge to fill the crib with stuffed animals or pillows, as tempting as it may be. While cuddly, they can pose a suffocation risk for newborns. Here are some additional tips to ensure the safest sleep environment for your baby:

- **Skip the pillows and bumpers:** Experts recommend against using pillows and crib bumpers for babies. Pillows can increase the risk of suffocation, and bumpers can trap heat and restrict airflow.

- **Back is best:** Always place your baby on their back to sleep, which is the safest position to reduce the risk of Sudden Infant Death Syndrome (SIDS). We know SIDS can be a scary term, but following safe sleep practices is the most important thing you can do to reduce this risk.

- **Stay cool:** Avoid overheating your baby. Dress them in lightweight clothing and keep the room temperature comfortable but not too warm.

- **Smoke-free zone:** Fresh air is key to a restful night's sleep for everyone, including your little one! To create a fresh and healthy sleep environment, avoid secondhand smoke. This includes smoke from cigarettes, cigars, pipes, and even e-cigarettes. Clean air helps your baby's lungs develop properly and allows them to breathe easily.

- **Consider a baby monitor:** While not essential, a baby monitor can provide peace of mind, especially in the early months. Choose one with clear sound quality and a secure connection to avoid any interference. Remember, a baby monitor is a tool, not a substitute for checking your baby regularly.

- **Soothing sounds:** Consider using a white noise machine or app to create a calming atmosphere. White noise can help mask distracting sounds and create a more peaceful sleep environment for your baby. Some babies find the shushing or nature sounds helpful as well. Keep the volume low and place the machine outside the crib.

A safe sleep space is a happy (and well-rested) baby! By following these simple tips, you can create a cozy and secure haven for your little one to thrive.

Beyond Safety: A World of Stimulation for Curious Minds

Now that you've created a safe haven for your little explorer, it's time to fill their world with wonder! Babies are like tiny sponges, soaking up information from everything around them. Let's create an environment that stimulates their developing senses and ignites their curiosity.

Flood their world with light, both natural and soft. Open the curtains whenever possible and let the sunshine bathe the room in a warm glow. Soft lamps can be just as effective when natural light isn't available. But don't stop at sight! Introduce them to a symphony of textures. Hang a colorful mobile that sways gently in the breeze, crinkle some interesting fabrics with different textures (think soft fleece, bumpy chenille, or crinkly paper), or place a safe, soft toy with contrasting patterns in their crib for them to explore.

Sound plays a vital role in their development too. Play some gentle music that is calming and soothing to their ears. Consider natural sounds like babbling brooks or soft rain, or classical melodies known for their calming effect. The sound of your voice, however, is the sweetest melody of all. Talk to them about your day, share your excitement about meeting them soon, or sing them a lullaby. They might not understand the words yet, but the love and warmth in your voice will be a source of immense comfort and a foundation for strong emotional bonds.

Here are some additional ideas you can sprinkle in:

- **High-contrast images:** Hang black and white or high-contrast images on the wall near their changing table or crib. Newborns can see best in black and white and high contrast, so these simple images will capture their attention.
- **Mobiles with different shapes and textures:** While mobiles with animals or familiar objects are cute, consider adding one with geometric shapes or interesting textures to provide a wider variety of visual stimulation.
- **Organic materials:** Create a warm and inviting space that's kind to the planet. Opt for woven baskets for storage, wooden furniture with clean lines, and organic cotton bedding. These natural materials are not only aesthetically pleasing but also promote healthy sleep and sustainable practices.

Healthy Choices for Pregnancy

Embarking on parenthood is a remarkable journey for your entire family unit. It's a time brimming with anticipation, a touch of nervous excitement, and an abundance of love. As you prepare for your little one's arrival, the choices you make now, especially regarding nutrition, have a significant impact on both of you and your developing baby.

A balanced diet rich in fruits, vegetables, and whole grains becomes even more crucial during pregnancy. This ensures both caregivers receive the essential vitamins and minerals needed for their own health, while also providing the building blocks for the baby's growth. Include a variety of protein sources, healthy fats, and whole grains to create a well-rounded dietary plan that benefits everyone involved in this shared experience.

Here are some additional considerations to optimize your nutritional well-being:

- **Prenatal Vitamins:** Consult with a healthcare professional to discuss the need for prenatal vitamins. These supplements can help ensure both the parent carrying the baby and the developing baby receive essential nutrients that may be difficult to obtain through diet alone, such as folic acid and iron.
- **Planning and Preparation:** Planning meals and prepping healthy snacks in advance can help caregivers avoid unhealthy choices when short on time or energy. This collaborative effort fosters shared responsibility and allows both parents to make informed dietary decisions.
- **Food Sensitivities:** If either caregiver has food sensitivities, discussing these with a healthcare professional is essential. Adjustments to the dietary plan can be made to accommodate these sensitivities and ensure both parents maintain optimal health.

It's normal to experience cravings during pregnancy. However, finding healthy alternatives whenever possible is beneficial. For example, if a craving for sweets arises, opt for fruit with a dollop of yogurt or a homemade fruit smoothie. Open communication between caregivers allows for collaborative decision-making when navigating cravings and finding healthy substitutes.

Listening to hunger and fullness cues is crucial. Skipping meals or feeling pressured to "eat for two" is not recommended. Aim for balanced, regular meals and healthy snacks throughout the day to ensure both caregivers feel nourished and energized.

Meal planning, grocery shopping, and cooking can be a fun way for caregivers to bond during pregnancy. Shared involvement in these tasks ensures both parents are familiar with healthy choices and can support each other's dietary needs. This collaborative approach fosters a sense of teamwork and shared responsibility for the well-being of the entire family unit.

Staying Hydrated is Essential: Aim for eight glasses of water a day, adjusting based on your climate and activity level. Proper hydration also aids digestion and nutrient absorption, making it even more important during pregnancy. Your body's working overtime to nurture new life, so listen to your thirst cues and don't hesitate to have extra water when needed.

Exercise can be a fantastic way to boost your mood and overall well-being during this exciting time. It doesn't have to be anything strenuous. Consider taking brisk walks together, exploring prenatal yoga classes as a couple (which can be particularly beneficial for the parent carrying the baby), or simply doing some gentle stretches at home. The key is to find activities you both enjoy and that make you feel good. Your body is changing rapidly, so listen to your limits and consult with a healthcare professional before starting a new exercise routine.

Throughout this shared experience, you might feel a range of emotions – excitement about meeting your little one, a touch of nervousness about the unknown, and a strong desire to connect with the baby growing inside you. As the parent carrying the baby, your body will undergo incredible transformations. The other caregiver can be a pillar of support by sharing in the excitement, helping with tasks around the house, and simply being there to listen and offer a loving presence.

No matter how you choose to embark on this parenthood journey, remember that you're in it together. By making healthy choices and prioritizing well-being, with a particular focus on the needs of the parent carrying the baby, you're creating a foundation for a happy and healthy start for both you and your soon-to-be little one.

The Stage is Set, Now Let the Connection Begin!

You've created a haven of comfort and stimulation, a world brimming with possibilities for your little explorer. But as parents, we know there's so much more to nurturing a happy, healthy child than just the physical environment. The most important foundation you can build for your baby isn't made of bricks or painted with colorful murals – it's the invisible thread of emotional connection that starts right now.

In the next section, we'll delve into the fascinating world of your baby's emotional development. We'll explore the power of your touch, the magic of your voice, and the simple ways you can start building a strong, secure attachment that will serve as a lifelong wellspring of love and security. This bond is the bedrock upon which your child's confidence, resilience, and social skills will flourish. It's the foundation for those bright minds we're all so excited to nurture!

So, take a deep breath, savor this precious time of anticipation, and get ready to embark on a whole new adventure – the adventure of building a deep and lasting connection with your little one. It might not always be sunshine and rainbows (we'll be honest, there will be a few diaper explosions along the way!), but the journey of parenthood is filled with moments of pure magic, and it all begins right here, right now, with this incredible bond.

In Action: The Power of Presence 

✓ **A Father's Lullaby:** John and Emily were eagerly anticipating the arrival of their first child. John, a natural worrier, felt a pang of anxiety about his ability to connect with such a tiny human. He wasn't sure how to sing lullabies or coo in a soothing voice. But Emily, a natural caregiver, gently suggested he simply talk to their baby in his regular voice. Every night, before bed, John would sit by the crib, recounting his day, sharing his excitement about meeting their little one, or simply singing silly songs he made up on the spot. To his surprise, the baby would often quiet down and focus on his voice, their eyes locked in a silent conversation. This nightly ritual became a foundation for their bond, and John's initial anxieties melted away as he discovered the power of his presence and connection.

✓ **A Grandparent's Embrace:** After their daughter gave birth, Michael and Susan welcomed the role of grandparents with open arms. They helped with household chores, offered emotional support to their daughter, and most importantly, showered their new grandchild with love. Susan, an artist, would create simple black and white drawings with bold lines and hang them near the crib. Michael, a retired musician, would hum calming melodies and sing old folk songs in a gentle voice. Despite not being the biological parents, their presence filled the baby's world with warmth and stimulation. This focus on connection, rather than traditional childcare activities, played a crucial role in building a strong and secure attachment between the grandparents and their grandchild.

Mindful Parenting: Sensory Play & Anticipation 

✓ **Introduction:** Welcome to your journey of mindful parenting! This section offers journaling prompts designed to help you cultivate calm, connect with your child, and navigate the ups and downs of parenthood. Take a few quiet moments whenever you feel the need to reflect and fill these spaces as you journey through this book. There's no right or wrong way to answer them. Simply let your thoughts and feelings flow freely on the page. A few starting prompts are below.

✓ **Pause & Reflect:**

- How can you create a more stimulating environment for your baby's senses?
- Imagine the moment you first meet your baby. Describe the emotions you anticipate feeling. How can you cultivate those feelings now?

Mindful Parenting: Sensory Play & Anticipation

Building the Bond:
The Roots of Emotional Connection

Congratulations, expecting parents! A joyful anticipation likely buzzes through you both. But amidst the preparations and checklists, there's another powerful emotion swirling around: a deep desire to connect with this tiny miracle growing inside one of you.

Imagine your baby bump as a tiny recipient of your love. Have you considered talking to your baby bump? It might sound funny at first, but it's a beautiful way to start building a connection. Whisper sweet nothings, share your hopes and dreams for their future — maybe becoming a world-famous musician or the kindest doctor (though their own path will undoubtedly be just as amazing!). Or simply sing a lullaby, your voice becoming a familiar and comforting melody. This early exposure calms them once they arrive, recognizing a sound that's been a constant source of comfort throughout their development.

The parent carrying the baby has a unique opportunity to bond through frequent touch. Gently stroke your belly as your baby kicks, a tender dance of anticipation. Place a loving hand on your bump as you talk, or create a shared musical experience by playing calming music and gently resting headphones on your belly. These simple acts create a physical connection and build a foundation of love.

Let's be honest, creating a whole new life can be a little nerve-wracking! Sharing your anxieties and excitement with your partner is incredibly comforting. Talk about your hopes for parenthood and the challenges you anticipate – maybe sleepless nights or endless diaper changes (but mostly the joy!). Discuss how you'll tackle them together as a team. You're in this incredible journey together, and building that sense of unity strengthens the foundation for your family.

Don't be afraid to involve others in this bonding process. Let grandparents, siblings, or close friends gently touch your belly and talk to your baby. Surrounding your little one with love and positive energy even before they arrive fosters a sense of security and belonging.

Building this bond takes time and doesn't have to be complicated. The simple act of acknowledging your baby's presence, talking to them, singing to them, and offering gentle touches all contribute to a strong foundation for a happy and healthy relationship. This connection will be the bedrock upon which you'll build trust, communication, and a lifetime of love with your child. The journey to parenthood officially begins with this invisible thread, and as your baby grows, so will this powerful bond you're nurturing right now.

The incredible bond you're nurturing right now is the cornerstone of a loving and supportive relationship with your child. It's a truly special time! But as you prepare for your little wonder's arrival, it's natural to wonder how you'll handle all the emotions that come with parenthood.

We all know there will be moments of frustration, meltdowns (yours!), and maybe even a few late-night "what am I doing wrong?" worries (totally normal, we promise!). The good news is, that there are tools and strategies you can learn to navigate these trickier moments and build a strong, happy relationship with your little one.

That's why the next section of this guide is called "Building Your Emotional Toolkit." Think of it as your parenting toolbox, filled with practical tips and techniques that can help you stay calm, connected, and confident even when things get a little crazy. From managing your own emotions to fostering cooperation and building communication, we'll equip you with the tools you need to thrive on this incredible journey.

So, take a deep breath, expecting parents! You've got this amazing foundation of love growing, and we're here to help you build a strong emotional toolkit to face parenthood with confidence.

In Action: Creative Ways to Bond Before Birth 

- ✓ **Dads and Dance Parties:** John, a self-proclaimed dancing machine, found connecting with his unborn baby through movement. Every evening, he'd put on upbeat music, place a hand on his belly, and sway gently from side to side. He even encouraged his partner to join in, turning their living room into a pre-parenthood dance party. This playful ritual filled their home with laughter and joy, creating a positive and interactive environment for their baby.

✓ Reading Rainbow: Maria, a bookworm at heart, decided to share her love of literature with her unborn child. Every night, she'd curl up with a comforting book and read aloud in a soothing voice. The rhythmic flow of the words and the gentle sounds of her voice created a calming routine that both Maria and her baby looked forward to. This act of reading not only fostered a love for language but also built a strong connection.

Make it Happen: Activities for Expecting Parents 

✓ Introduction: The "Make it Happen" section offers practical steps to turn the concepts of building an emotional bond with your child into tangible actions. Here, you'll find simple yet meaningful activities you can incorporate into your daily routine. Remember, every little gesture counts in nurturing that powerful connection.

✓ Activities:
  - Start a bedtime story routine: Read aloud to your partner's belly, creating a calming ritual and introducing your baby to the wonderful world of stories.
  - Create a "welcome home" basket: Fill a basket with cozy blankets, soft toys, and baby essentials, allowing you to focus on the positive anticipation of your baby's arrival.
  - Write a letter to your unborn baby: Express your love, hopes, and dreams for their future.

The Gift of Time:
Building Your Emotional Toolkit for Parenthood

You're about to embark on an incredible adventure of creating and nurturing a whole new life. A beautiful cascade of emotions – excitement, joy, maybe even a touch of nervousness about meeting your soon-to-be-born child – is perfectly natural. But amidst the baby clothes shopping and nursery decorating, take a moment to consider the most powerful tools you already possess: yourselves.

Imagine yourselves as explorers setting sail on an uncharted adventure, with the most precious treasure waiting for you at the end – your little one's first smile, their tiny coos, those amazing developmental leaps. But unexpected storms await too – sleepless nights, cranky cries, and maybe even a few meltdowns (yours, not the baby's…yet!).

The key to navigating this beautiful chaos lies in building your emotional toolkit. An emotional toolkit refers to a collection of personal strategies and resources that help you manage your emotions effectively. It's like a toolbox filled with different tools you can use depending on the situation. Here are some examples of what might be included in an emotional toolkit for parenthood:

- **Self-awareness:** Being able to recognize your own emotions and how they might be impacting your thoughts and behaviors. To develop self-awareness, you can start a journaling practice. Note down your emotions throughout the day and any situations that triggered them. Reflect on how these emotions might be affecting your thoughts and actions. This will help you identify patterns and become more aware of your emotional triggers as you prepare to welcome your child.

- **Coping mechanisms:** Healthy ways to deal with stress, frustration, or anger. To build healthy coping mechanisms, explore relaxation techniques like deep breathing or meditation (there are many free guided meditations available online or through apps). Consider activities you already enjoy, like taking walks in nature or listening to calming music, and incorporate them into your routine as stress relievers. These healthy habits will be even more important once your little one arrives.

- **Communication skills:** The ability to express your needs and feelings clearly and listen attentively to your partner and child. To strengthen your communication skills, practice open and honest communication with your partner. Discuss your hopes, fears, and expectations for parenthood. Role-play different scenarios that might arise, like managing disagreements or handling a crying baby. Actively listen to each other and validate each other's feelings. Strong communication will be essential as you build a loving bond with your soon-to-be-born child.

- **Empathy:** The ability to understand and share your child's feelings. To build empathy, read books or articles about child development. This will help you understand the emotional stages your baby will go through and how to respond to their needs in a sensitive way. Consider your own childhood experiences and how they might shape your parenting approach as you prepare to meet your little one.

- **Positive self-talk:** Encouraging yourself with positive affirmations instead of negative self-criticism. To cultivate positive self-talk, challenge negative thoughts with positive reframing. For example, instead of thinking "I'm going to be a terrible parent," reframe it to "Parenting is a learning experience, and I'm committed to doing my best for my child." Surround yourself with supportive people who uplift and encourage you. A positive mindset will be invaluable as you embark on this exciting journey of parenthood.

- **Problem-solving skills:** The ability to identify problems, brainstorm solutions, and make decisions that work for your family. To hone your problem-solving skills, practice brainstorming solutions together as a couple. When faced with a challenge, discuss various options and weigh the pros and cons of each. There's no one-size-fits-all approach to parenthood, so find what works best for your unique family dynamic as you raise your expected child.

Building an emotional toolkit for parenthood is an ongoing process. As your child grows and develops, you'll encounter new challenges and emotions that will require different tools. But by starting to build your toolkit now, you'll be well-equipped to navigate the joys and challenges of parenthood with confidence and resilience, ready to provide a loving and supportive environment for your soon-to-be-born child.

Nurturing the Connection: A Journey Before Birth

Pregnancy isn't just about physical preparation for expecting parents; it's a beautiful gift of nine months to cultivate a lifelong connection with your child. These early months are a dance between cherishing the present and the exciting anticipation of the future. As your baby grows inside one caregiver, a sense of wonder blossoms for everyone involved.

The urge to connect might manifest in a variety of ways. This could involve talking to your baby bump, singing lullabies together, or sharing stories about the exciting life that awaits your little one. These gentle interactions spark a connection, a familiarity that transcends words. Your baby might even respond with a flutter or a kick, a tiny movement that sends shivers of excitement down your spine, a magical moment for both of you.

This time is also an invitation for both caregivers to reflect inwards. Review your own childhood experiences. Did you have nurturing caregivers who showered you with love and support? Or perhaps your upbringing fuels a desire to create a different environment for your own child. Although you'll be raising them, your child is not an extension of you or your partner. They'll be their own unique person, with their own personality, quirks, and passions. It's about embracing this individuality while offering your unwavering love and guidance as parents-to-be.

From Expectations to Intentions: Shaping the Parent You Want to Be

The pregnancy journey can be an emotional rollercoaster. Excitement bubbles over, joy fills your heart, and maybe a sprinkle of nervousness flutters in your stomach. It's natural to have expectations about parenthood, but here's a secret: the most empowering shift you can make is from expectations to intentions. Don't just picture picture-perfect moments (because let's be honest, those are rarely the reality!). Instead, focus on the kind of parent you want to be.

What values do you want to be the cornerstones of your family? How can you create a safe space where your child feels free to express themself and grow emotionally? How will you communicate with them, fostering an open and honest dialogue that strengthens your bond? By reflecting on your own experiences, both positive and negative, you can learn from the past and pave the way for a more fulfilling parenting journey.

Even before their first cry, your baby's story is already unfolding. It's a story of miraculous growth, of a spirit waiting to meet the amazing people who will be their parents. By acknowledging your feelings and desires, you're approaching parenthood with intention and responsibility. You're building a foundation for a truly special relationship, a bond nurtured with love and understanding right from the very beginning. You're not alone in this incredible adventure. Lean on your partner, seek out support networks, and embrace the joys and challenges that come along the way. This is more than just preparing for parenthood; it's about creating a love story that will unfold and grow throughout your lives together.

From Toolbelt to Teamwork: Embracing the Wonder Years

Equipped with the knowledge of your emotional toolkit, now it's time to start putting those tools to good use. Parenthood is a beautiful learning experience, filled with both sunshine and unexpected rain showers. But fear not, you're not alone!

Here's where things get exciting! In this next part of the book, we'll dive headfirst into the fascinating world of your baby's development. We'll explore the incredible milestones they'll reach, from those first precious coos to taking their very first wobbly steps. We'll also unveil the secret language of your little one – understanding their cries, coos, and gurgles becomes your superpower, helping you decipher their needs and build a strong, connected bond.

So, take a deep breath, expecting parents, and get ready for the adventure to truly begin! We're here to guide you every step of the way, celebrating the highs and offering support through the inevitable challenges. You've got this!

In Action: Building the Bond Before Birth 

✓ **The Doodling Duo:** Emily and Michael, expecting their first child, were both artistic souls. They couldn't wait to share their love of creativity with their little one. Every evening, they'd settle down together, each with a sketchbook. Michael would create whimsical drawings, imagining adventures he and his child would have together. Emily, inspired by the growing life within her, would sketch gentle, flowing lines, symbolizing the love and nurturing environment they'd create. They'd often talk about their drawings, narrating stories and sharing dreams for their future family. This artistic ritual not only fostered a creative connection but also became a way for them to express their anticipation and excitement for parenthood.

✓ **The Lullaby Legacy:** Elena, of Greek heritage, was raised in a large, musical family, and cherished the tradition of singing lullabies passed down through generations. Now pregnant with her first child, she longed to create a similar legacy. Every night, she'd sit comfortably and sing a variety of lullabies in her native Greek. Sometimes, she'd even create her melodies, whispering sweet nothings and promises of love to her unborn baby. Her husband, David, initially felt a little self-conscious about joining in. However, seeing Elena's joy and the calming effect it had on their baby (judging by the reduced movement), he overcame his shyness. Soon, they were singing duets, filling their home with music, and creating a special bedtime routine that connected them all.

Make it Happen: Activities for a Confident Start 

✓ Level Up Your Parenthood:
- **Take a parenting class together:** Enroll in a prenatal or new parent education class to gain valuable knowledge and connect with other expecting parents.
- **Create a self-care routine:** Schedule time for activities that help you relax and de-stress, like reading, taking a bath, or spending time in nature.
- **Practice relaxation techniques:** Explore deep breathing exercises, meditation, or mindfulness practices to manage stress and anxiety.
- **Build your support network:** Connect with other parents, friends, or family members who can offer emotional support and practical help.

66

"Children are not things to be molded, but are people to be unfolded."

- JESS LAIR
(Early childhood education advocate)

Part 2:

Deciphering the Cries: Understanding Your Wondrous Wonder Years

Inside This Part

The anticipation is building! You've diligently prepared for your little miracle's arrival, and now you're about to embark on the amazing adventure of getting to know them. Part 1 equipped you for this exciting time, guiding you through their miraculous prenatal development and fostering that beautiful bond even before birth.

But don't worry, even without instruction manuals, you can learn to understand your little one! This part of the book is your decoder ring for navigating the wondrous wonder years, helping you decipher those tiny cries that might seem like a foreign language at first.

This is a journey you're taking together. Part 2 will equip you with the tools to understand your baby's unique language, nurture their development, and build a foundation of love and connection that will endure and grow alongside your child. So, take a deep breath, expecting parents, and get ready to unlock the magic of those wondrous wonder years!

Witnessing Your Baby's Growth: *Understanding Your Baby's Development*

The moment your baby arrives is a surge of emotions – pure joy, awe, and maybe a touch of surprise at those tiny features you've only imagined. But amidst the initial flurry, a new adventure begins: witnessing your child's incredible development.

From the very first breath, your baby embarks on a journey of discovery. Their senses are overwhelmed with new information – the bright lights of the nursery contrasting with the comforting warmth of your skin, the unfamiliar sounds of the world replacing the muffled hush they knew before. In those early weeks, their cries are their primary way of communicating. Unlike other baby animals who are born with some ability to care for themselves, human babies are entirely dependent on you, their caregivers. This crying might sound like a constant chorus at times, but it's their only way to signal a need.

It might be hunger, a dirty diaper, discomfort from being too hot or cold, or simply a desire for your closeness. Your job in these early days is to decipher these cries and respond with love and care. It's a beautiful dance of learning each other's cues, and while it may not always be easy, understanding your baby's needs is key to building a strong bond. Rest assured, your baby isn't crying to make you frustrated; they're simply trying to communicate in the only way they know how. As you learn their language of cries, whimpers, and coos, you'll witness the incredible progress they make each day. This is the beginning of a remarkable journey, and you're right there at the heart of it all.

As your baby grows and develops, those early cries will transform into a delightful symphony of gurgles, coos, and babbles. It's their way of reaching out, connecting with you, and starting a conversation. But how do you decipher this new language? Don't worry, you're not expected to be a baby whisperer just yet! In the next section, we'll explore the amazing world of baby talk and discover how playtime can be your secret weapon for understanding your little one's needs and fostering a strong bond. Get ready for some giggles, some silly faces, and a whole lot of fun – because play is more than just entertainment, it's the foundation for communication and learning in those precious early months.

In Action: Nurturing Language in Young Children 

✓ The Language Barrier: Anya and Kai welcomed their bilingual baby, Maya, into the world. Anya spoke primarily English at home, while Kai spoke Farsi. They worried that their multilingual environment might confuse or delay Maya's language development. However, their pediatrician reassured them that exposure to multiple languages is beneficial. Anya and Kai embraced this advice, consistently speaking their respective languages to Maya throughout the day. While it took Maya a little longer to start babbling compared to some of her peers, she eventually surprised everyone by speaking both English and Farsi fluently by the age of two.

✓ The Playful Talkers: Maria and Luis were concerned about their 18-month-old twins, Mateo and Isabella. While the twins babbled constantly, they weren't yet using many words. Maria and Luis worried they might be falling behind in their language development.

However, a speech-language pathologist (SLP) reassured them that Mateo and Isabella were on track. The SLP explained that some twins prioritize communication through gestures and play before focusing on spoken language. The SLP recommended incorporating more singing, rhyming, and interactive play into their routines. They suggested using simple picture books and pointing out objects, encouraging the twins to label them.

Maria and Luis began incorporating playful activities like peek-a-boo, singing action songs, and building simple structures with blocks. They also narrated their daily activities, describing objects and actions. Within a few months, Mateo and Isabella blossomed verbally. They started using single words, then short phrases, mimicking what they heard and excitedly labeling things around them.

Mindful Parenting: Baby Bond Reflections

✓ **Pause & Reflect:**

- Describe a recent milestone your baby achieved. How did it make you feel?
- How does your baby communicate with you?
- What are your favorite things to do with your baby?
- What are you looking forward to at this stage in your baby's development?

Unlocking Your Baby's Language:
Communication Through Play

You've likely spent hours decorating the nursery, picking out the cutest outfits, and maybe even reading up on all the latest baby development milestones. But have you considered how you'll communicate with your little miracle before they can speak your language?

While it might seem like coos and gurgles are just adorable noises, they're actually your baby's first attempts to connect with you. This exciting section will show you how to unlock the magic of baby talk and how playtime becomes your secret weapon for understanding your baby's needs and building a strong bond.

Think of your baby as a tiny explorer entering a world bursting with new sights, sounds, and sensations. They don't have words to express their wonder, frustration, or excitement – that's where you come in! Playtime becomes a beautiful conversation, a dance of silly faces, playful sounds, and gentle touches. Here's how it works:

- **Mirror, Mirror on the Wall:** The Science Behind Facial Fascination. Newborns are captivated by faces. Studies suggest this fascination stems from a need to understand human emotions and social cues. Make funny expressions, sing silly songs in high-pitched voices, and observe your baby's response. This playful imitation not only entertains them but also demonstrates the joy of communication and the power of facial expressions.

- **The Power of Touch:** More Than Just Comfort. Skin-to-skin contact is incredibly calming for newborns. Cuddling your baby close, gently stroking their cheek, or giving them a soothing massage goes beyond comfort. These gentle touches establish a sense of security and trust – the foundation for a strong bond. Research shows that skin-to-skin contact can regulate a baby's heart rate, breathing, and temperature, promoting a sense of calm and well-being.

- **Sing a Song of Everything:** The Musicality of Language. You don't need to be a professional singer! Narrate your day in a sing-song voice as you change their diaper or dress them. The rhythmic sounds and the inflection in your voice not only capture their attention but also help them learn the flow of language. Experts believe this musicality plays a crucial role in language development. By incorporating variations in pitch and rhythm, you're exposing your baby to the building blocks of spoken language.

- **A Symphony of Objects:** Everyday Sounds Spark Curiosity. The world is full of fascinating sounds for your baby. Shake a rattle, crinkle a soft blanket, or tap a spoon on a highchair tray. These everyday objects transform into instruments in your playful orchestra, sparking their curiosity and helping them understand cause and effect. Varying the sounds not only keeps them engaged but also introduces them to the concept of manipulating their environment to create sounds.

As you engage in playful moments with your baby, remember that playtime is a two-way street. It's your chance to connect, learn their unique language, and build a strong foundation for communication and a loving bond that will grow and strengthen over time.

Throughout playtime, narrate your baby's actions and feelings. Is that a gurgle of curiosity as they reach for the brightly colored rattle? Is that a fussy cry because they're feeling overwhelmed by all the new sights and sounds? By putting words to their experiences, you help them connect sounds with experiences, laying the groundwork for language development.

Playtime isn't a monologue; a precious exchange of playful sounds. After making a silly sound or singing a song in a high-pitched voice, wait expectantly for your baby's response. It might be a gurgle, a coo, or a kick – all are their way of joining the conversation. This call and response not only keeps them engaged but also teaches them the rhythm of back-and-forth communication.

Just like you wouldn't shout at a sleepy baby, tailor your playfulness to their mood. If they're fussy, use calming tones, gentle touches, and soft lullabies. If they're excited and kicking their legs with glee, respond with big smiles, energetic coos, and playful bounces. Mirroring their energy creates a sense of connection and shows them that you're paying attention to their cues.

Pay close attention to what captures your baby's interest. Do their eyes light up at the sound of a particular song? Do they reach out and grab at the high-contrast patterns on a black-and-white book? Use their preferences to guide your playtime activities, making it even more engaging and stimulating for them.

Playtime is a sensory feast for your baby. Offer them safe teething toys with various textures to explore, crinkle a colorful fabric book to introduce them to the sound, or blow bubbles for them to chase and giggle at. These sensory experiences not only spark their curiosity but also provide opportunities for communication through their delighted expressions and happy vocalizations.

As your baby develops, celebrate their communication milestones with excitement and praise. Did they make eye contact for the first time during playtime? Did they reach for your finger during a silly song? Acknowledging these advancements shows them you notice their progress and encourages them to continue interacting with you. This positive reinforcement strengthens the connection you're building and lets them know that communication is a joyful experience. Playtime becomes a safe space for them to experiment with sounds, gestures, and facial expressions, all while knowing they have your full attention and encouragement. These early interactions are the building blocks for a lifetime of communication. So put on your playful hat, embrace the giggles and gurgles, and get ready to discover the magic of baby talk together. The more you engage in playful conversations, the stronger your bond will become, and the sooner you'll be deciphering the fascinating language of your little one.

Every Baby's a Chatty Charlie (or Cherie): Decoding Your Unique Communicator

Playtime becomes a safe space for them to experiment with sounds, gestures, and facial expressions, all while knowing they have your full attention and encouragement. These early interactions spark a lifelong journey of communication, and each baby's language is unique. Just like adults have different accents, personalities, and ways of expressing themselves, so too will your baby develop their communication style. Here are some tips to help you decipher your little one's unique language:

- **Become a Baby Whisperer:** Pay close attention to their cries. A hungry cry will sound different from a tired cry or a cry for attention. The pitch, intensity, and duration of their cries can offer clues to their needs.

- **Body Language Bonanza:** Don't underestimate the power of body language! Is your baby arching their back and stiffening their body? This might indicate discomfort. Are they turning their head away or fussing when you try to change their diaper? They might be expressing displeasure. Observe their body language alongside their vocalizations for a fuller picture.

- **The Power of Repetition:** It's a learning process for both! When your baby makes a sound or gesture that seems to communicate a specific need, repeat it back to them in a playful way. This reinforces the connection between the sound/gesture and their desire.

- **Be Patient, Detective Parent:** Cracking your baby's communication code takes time and practice. Don't get discouraged if you don't understand them right away. The more time you spend interacting and observing them, the better you'll become at deciphering their unique language.

So put on your playful hat, embrace the giggles and gurgles, and get ready to discover the magic of baby talk together. The more you engage in playful conversations, the stronger your bond will become, and the sooner you'll be deciphering the fascinating language of your little one.

But what if happy coos turn to frustrated cries? Every parent experiences those tearful moments, and sometimes it can feel overwhelming. In the next section, we'll shift gears and explore the world of emotions. We'll delve into the fascinating (and sometimes messy!) world of baby emotions, equipping you with soothing techniques and the power of empathy to navigate those stormy moments. We'll learn how to help your little one weather tantrums, understand their feelings, and build the emotional intelligence that sets them up for success. So take a deep breath, new parent, you've got this! We're here to guide you through the giggles, the tears, and everything in between.

In Action: Understanding Your Baby 

✓ **The Mystery of the Cries:** Lisa, a first-time mom, felt a pit of worry growing in her stomach every time her newborn son, Ethan, cried. She desperately wanted to soothe him but struggled to decipher his cries. Feeling defeated, Lisa confided in her pediatrician. The doctor reassured her that all babies cry, and it's their primary way of communicating. The pediatrician recommended paying attention to Ethan's cues — facial expressions, body language, and the quality of his cries. With practice, Lisa became more attuned to Ethan's unique cries. The short, sharp cry meant hunger, while the long, wailing cry indicated tiredness. Lisa also noticed that Ethan calmed down quickly when she responded to his hunger cues with breastfeeding but needed a rocking motion and white noise to soothe him when he was tired. By deciphering Ethan's cries, Lisa gained confidence in her parenting abilities and developed a secure bond with her son.

✓ **The Signing Success Story:** Michael and Jessica were eager to find ways to communicate with their daughter, Lily, before she could speak. They decided to try baby sign language. At first, they felt a bit silly waving their hands and signing basic words like "milk" and "more," but Lily quickly grasped the concept. Within months, Lily started using signs to express her needs and wants. This not only reduced frustration on both sides but also fostered a sense of connection and empowerment in Lily. As Lily's verbal skills developed, she continued to use signs alongside spoken words, eventually transitioning to all spoken language. Michael and Jessica were pleased with their decision to introduce sign language, believing it had accelerated Lily's communication development and strengthened their parent-child bond.

Make it Happen: Activities for Connection & Growth 

✓ **Level Up Your Parenthood:**
- **Take a baby sign language class:** Learning a few basic signs can be a fun and effective way to communicate with your baby before they can speak.
- **Narrate your day:** Talk to your baby throughout the day, describing your actions and the world around them. This constant flow of language helps with brain development and vocabulary building.
- **Create a baby book:** Document your baby's milestones and special moments with photos, notes, and observations. This can be a helpful tool for tracking their progress.

Fostering Emotional Regulation: Soothing Techniques and Empathy

The nursery gleams, a picture of meticulous planning. Tiny onesies, adorably folded, promise endless cuddles. Yet, amidst the excitement, a question lingers: how will you navigate the emotional world of your newborn wonder?

Newborns may not speak, but they cry – a powerful language expressing hunger, fatigue, discomfort, or simply being overwhelmed by a world of dazzling lights, loud noises, and unfamiliar textures. Here's your superpower: empathy. Imagine yourself in a sea of such sensations. No wonder they cry!

Understanding Their Cries: This understanding is key to calming them down. Validate their feelings, building a strong emotional connection. The next time tears flow try phrases like, "It's okay to feel frustrated, little one. We're here to help you calm down." Or, if there's a loud noise, "Those loud noises can be scary! Let's find a quieter spot to cuddle."

These simple phrases show you understand and are there to comfort them.

Soothing Techniques: Now, let's explore your comforting toolkit:
- **The Power of Touch:** I know this might sound repetitive, but skin-to-skin contact, often called kangaroo care, is so crucial for your baby's well-being that it deserves constant emphasis. Skin-to-skin contact can be incredibly calming. Hold your baby close, chest to chest, and let them feel your warmth and heartbeat. Swaddling can also mimic the feeling of being held and provide security.
- **Rhythmic Movement:** The gentle sway of a rocking chair or the rhythmic patting of your back can be very soothing. Experiment with different movements to see what works best for your unique baby.
- **Calming Sounds:** As suggested before, white noise can be a lifesaver. It mimics the sounds they heard in the womb and can be very calming. Try a white noise machine, a nature sounds recording, or even the shushing sound of your own voice.
- **Sucking Reflex:** Some babies find comfort in sucking. Offer a pacifier or let them suck on your clean finger.

There's no one-size-fits-all approach. Experiment and find what works best for your baby. Be patient, attentive, and responsive to their cues.

Remember, there's magic in your touch, your voice, and your presence. These are the building blocks of a secure attachment, the foundation for your baby's emotional well-being. In the next section, we'll explore the concept of gentle discipline. Here, we'll learn how to communicate boundaries with love and understanding, fostering cooperation in your little one without resorting to punishment or negativity.

In Action: Calming the Storm

✓ **The Sleepless Nights:** Emily, a single mom to newborn Lily, battled sleep deprivation. Lily cried inconsolably every night, leaving Emily feeling helpless. Exhausted and overwhelmed, Emily confided in her sister, who suggested a bedtime routine. Together they created a calming nighttime ritual – a warm bath, a gentle massage, and soft lullabies. Emily responded to Lily's cries with empathy and soothing techniques, like rocking and shushing, avoiding picking Lily up with every whimper. Within a few weeks, Lily's nighttime cries became less frequent and intense. The predictable routine and Emily's calm presence helped Lily feel safe and secure, allowing her to fall asleep more easily.

Mindful Parenting: Decoding Cues & Creating Calm

✓ **Pause & Reflect:**
- What are some of your baby's cues that indicate they are upset?
- Describe a recent situation where you struggled to calm your baby. What emotions did you experience?
- How can you create a more calming environment for your baby?
- What are some of your goals for helping your baby develop healthy sleep habits?
- Imagine yourself a year from now. What does a typical bedtime routine look like in your household?

Nurturing Foundations of Positive Behavior:
Building Communication Through Gentle Discipline

Those first few weeks with your newborn are a beautiful storm of emotions – pure, unadulterated love washes over you alongside moments of exhaustion and the occasional cry that leaves you feeling like a tiny human decoder ring is the key to survival. But amidst the diaper changes and late-night feedings, there's a beautiful opportunity to lay the groundwork for positive behavior and a secure connection. That's where gentle discipline comes in – a toolbox filled with strategies that don't involve shouting matches or punishment, but instead focus on understanding your baby's world and building a foundation of trust and love.

The Magic of Secure Attachment: Responsive Care as the Cornerstone

Before we delve into gentle discipline, let's explore the magic of secure attachment. This powerful bond forms between you and your baby through responsive care – the act of recognizing and responding to their cues with love and attention. Imagine your newborn as a brand new explorer, venturing into a world bursting with dazzling lights, loud noises, and unfamiliar textures. Every gurgle, coo, or cry is their way of communicating. They might be hungry, tired, uncomfortable, or simply overwhelmed and seeking your comforting presence.

By being responsive, you essentially translate this new language. You show your baby they're heard and cared for. This doesn't mean you have to be a superhero, responding to every whimper with lightning speed (though sometimes you might!). It means being attentive to their cues and responding in a timely and loving way. Think of it like a conversation – your baby communicates a need, and you respond with care and comfort.

The magic happens in these responsive interactions. By responding to your baby's needs, you build a powerful sense of trust and security. They learn that their cries and cues are acknowledged and addressed, fostering a feeling of safety and well-being. This foundation of secure attachment sets the stage for healthy emotional development, creating a secure base for them to explore the world with confidence. They know they have your love and support as they navigate their exciting new world.

There will be moments, of course when you feel like you're deciphering a code written in a foreign language. Don't worry, that's perfectly normal! This journey of responsive care is a two-way street – you'll learn from your baby as you decipher their cries, coos, and body language together, and they'll learn to feel safe and secure in your loving embrace. So cuddle close, respond with care, and witness the beautiful bond blossom between you and your little explorer. Celebrate the small victories, too! Did your baby finally calm down after feeding? Did they drift off to sleep nestled against you? These moments, though seemingly insignificant, are building blocks of trust and security, and a testament to your growing skills as responsive caregivers.

Building the Foundation: Gentle Redirection and Routines

Now that we understand the importance of secure attachment, let's explore how gentle discipline builds upon this foundation. Your newborn is on an incredible adventure – a journey of discovery filled with dazzling lights, fascinating sounds, and unfamiliar textures. It's a world that can be stimulating and overwhelming at times. They can't quite grasp complex instructions yet, and their impulses are still under development. This is where you come in, their guide and safe haven.

Setting realistic boundaries becomes crucial. Instead of resorting to punishment, which might leave them feeling confused and frustrated, focus on gentle redirection. Imagine your little explorer reaching for your glasses. With a soft touch, you can gently move their hand away and offer them a safe teether instead. This not only protects your glasses but also provides them with an appropriate outlet for their curiosity.

Creating predictable routines is another way to set your baby up for success. Think about it – a consistent schedule for sleep, feeding, and playtime helps them feel safe and secure. They know what to expect, which reduces frustration and allows them to focus on exploring the world around them. Imagine the comfort of a familiar bedtime story or the joy of a predictable playtime routine. These routines become anchors, a foundation of security that allows them to blossom.

As you cuddle your little explorer close and respond to their needs with care, you're laying the groundwork for a lifetime of positive communication. It's a beautiful dance – you learn their language of coos, cries, and body language, and they learn to trust you as a source of comfort and security. This foundation you're building now sets the stage for future interactions, where clear communication becomes even more important.

Of course, parenthood isn't always sunshine and snuggles. There will be moments when your baby's cries feel like a foreign language, and deciphering their needs can be a challenge. These routines and gentle redirection become the building blocks for future communication. In the next section, we'll delve deeper into some common concerns faced by new parents, all while keeping the principles of gentle discipline at the forefront. There's no such thing as a perfect parent, and setbacks are a normal part of the journey. With a little understanding and a toolbox full of practical tips, you'll be well on your way to conquering those everyday challenges and fostering a happy, secure connection with your little one.

In Action: Building with Trust

- ✓ **The Curious Climber:** Mark and Lisa were thrilled to witness their daughter Sofia's newfound mobility. Sofia was crawling with newfound confidence, eager to explore every corner of their home. However, this newfound independence came with challenges. Sofia was fascinated by electrical cords and considered the coffee table a prime climbing destination. Mark and Lisa found themselves constantly on edge, worried about

Sofia's safety. One day, a friend suggested gentle redirection. Instead of yelling "No!" or scolding Sofia, they implemented a system of positive reinforcement. When Sofia approached an off-limits area, they would gently redirect her to a safe play area filled with age-appropriate toys. They also "baby-proofed" their home by covering electrical outlets and securing furniture. Gradually, Sofia learned the boundaries of their home without feeling reprimanded or punished.

✓ **The Fussy Mealtimes:** David and Emily were at their wit's end. Mealtimes with their son, Ethan, had become a battleground of frustration. Ethan would reject any food they offered him, leaving them worried about his nutrition and feeling defeated. A pediatrician suggested focusing on creating a positive mealtime experience. They redesigned mealtimes to be a social event, letting Ethan explore his food with his hands and narrating their actions throughout the meal. They also offered Ethan a variety of textures and flavors, allowing him to experiment at his own pace. Over time, the pressure to eat disappeared, and Ethan began to show curiosity about trying new foods.

Conquering Everyday Challenges: Practical Strategies for Common Concerns

It's a beautiful, bewildering time, filled with exhaustion, wonder, and an overwhelming urge to protect this little miracle. But amidst the diaper changes and late-night feedings, there's an exciting opportunity. You're not just surviving, you're building a foundation – a foundation of communication, trust, and a love that will only grow stronger with each passing day. Let's navigate some common concerns together, and show you how to conquer those everyday challenges as a team.

Crying is a constant companion in those early days, and it's easy to feel overwhelmed by the symphony of wails that pierces the quiet night. Crying is your baby's main form of communication. They might be hungry, tired, uncomfortable, or simply seeking your comforting presence. Here's your toolbox: try rocking, singing a lullaby, swaddling your baby for warmth, or making gentle shushing sounds. Skin-to-skin contact can also be incredibly calming for newborns. If you've tried everything and your baby still seems inconsolable, don't be afraid to put them down safely in their crib and take a short break to gather yourself. You'll be better equipped to soothe them after a few minutes of self-care.

Sweet Dreams: Establishing Healthy Sleep Habits

Sleep – that glorious word that might now feel like a distant dream – is a common concern. Every baby is unique, and their sleep patterns will develop over time. Don't get discouraged by those first few interrupted nights filled with the glow of a monitor and the desperate search for a pacifier that mysteriously vanished under the crib (again!). Instead, focus on creating a calming bedtime routine that signals to your little one it's time to wind down. This could include a warm bath, a gentle massage, and some quiet cuddling. A consistent routine is key – even if those "nights" start to blend into long stretches!

Nourishing Your Baby: Breastfeeding, Bottle-Feeding, and Finding What Works for You

Mealtime, whether breastfeeding or bottle-feeding, comes with its own learning curve. Don't be afraid to ask for help from lactation consultants, nurses, or experienced parents. A fed and happy baby is a happy (and hopefully sleepy) baby. There's no shame in seeking support; a healthy and well-nourished little one is the ultimate goal.

Breastfeeding is a beautiful journey, but for some of us, it can also be a challenging one. My personal experience involved encountering difficulties with latching and milk supply, leading me to explore breast pumping as an alternative. While pumping provided the means to nourish my baby with breast milk, I soon realized I was making a common mistake – using the pump on one breast at a time.

This approach, while seemingly efficient at first, actually doubled my pumping time. It wasn't until later that I discovered the wonders of double-electric breast pumps! These pumps allow you to express milk from both breasts simultaneously, saving precious time and effort in your busy routine.

If you're considering using a breast pump, I highly recommend investing in a double electric pump from the very beginning. This will save you time and effort in the long run, and may even contribute to a more successful pumping experience. Remember, the decision to breastfeed or pump is personal. There's no right or wrong answer — the most important thing is to nourish your baby and find a method that works best for you and your family.

Supporting Your Baby's Development: A World of Discovery

The early months are a magical time filled with rapid growth and development for your little one. From strengthening their muscles to exploring their senses, each day brings new opportunities for learning and exploration. This section will equip you with strategies to nurture your baby's development through everyday activities.

Here are some key areas you can focus on:

- **Tummy Time:** Though it might sound intimidating, tummy time is simply placing your baby on their tummy for short periods throughout the day. This strengthens their neck and back muscles, crucial for rolling, crawling, and eventually sitting up. Tummy time doesn't have to be a struggle — place a colorful blanket or mirror under your baby to pique their curiosity.
- **Bath Time Fun:** Bath time can be a source of anxiety for new parents, but it's a great opportunity for bonding and playful interaction. Fill a small tub with warm water and use a gentle baby wash. No need for a full-body scrub-down every day — a quick sponge bath might be sufficient most of the time. Remember, water

safety is paramount – never leave your baby unattended in the tub. Beyond cleaning, bath time can be a stimulating sensory experience. Splash gently with your baby, sing songs, and use bath toys to encourage their exploration.

- **Soothing Tummy Troubles:** Gas pains can be a real source of discomfort for newborns. If you suspect your baby has gas, try gently massaging their tummy in a clockwise motion. Burping them frequently during feedings can also help release trapped air. Simple bicycle leg motions can also help relieve discomfort.
- **The Power of Play**: It's important to remember that play is crucial for your baby's development. From peek-a-boo to singing songs, even simple interactions stimulate their senses and cognitive skills.

Taking Care of Yourself: The Secret Weapon of Happy Babies

It's easy to get laser-focused on your baby's needs, but don't forget about yourselves! Taking care of yourself is the secret weapon of happy babies. Make sure you're getting enough sleep whenever possible, even if it means tag-teaming nighttime feedings with your partner. Eat healthy meals and snacks to keep your energy levels up. Don't be afraid to delegate tasks – ask your partner, family, or friends for help with errands or household chores. A happy and healthy parent is better equipped to care for their baby's needs.

Parenthood is a constant learning curve. Even with the best intentions and the most comprehensive knowledge, mistakes are an inevitable part of parenting. As we strive to follow every instruction and guideline, we risk feeling overwhelmed and incompetent in our role as caregivers. Parenting is not a science governed by rigid rules and formulas; it's an art that requires a balance of knowledge, intuition, and adaptability. While guidelines and expert advice can provide valuable support, they should not replace our innate ability to connect with our children and respond to their unique needs.

There's no such thing as a perfect parent. Trust your instincts, seek knowledge from reliable sources, and know that every experience, every challenge, is an opportunity to learn and grow alongside your baby.

Those newborn days melt away quickly, and soon your little one will be on the move! Buckle up, because the next part of the book – toddlerhood – is an exciting whirlwind of discovery, challenges, and those oh-so-adorable "firsts." We'll delve into the wonderful world of toddlers. We'll explore their developmental milestones, unlock the power of play in their learning journey, and equip you with practical tools for navigating tantrums, separation anxiety, and sleep issues. These early years are all about fostering emotional intelligence, building strong boundaries, and nurturing a sense of self-esteem in your little one. So, take a deep breath, embrace the adventure, and get ready to be amazed by the curious climber you helped create!

Make it Happen: Healthy Habits for Your Baby 

✓ Level Up Your Parenthood:
- **Develop a sleep schedule for your baby:** Create a consistent routine for bedtime, naptime, and wake-up time. This will help regulate your baby's sleep cycle and make it easier for them to fall asleep and stay asleep.
- **Create a calming bedtime routine:** This could include a warm bath, a gentle massage, soft lullabies, and rocking.
- **Establish a feeding routine:** Breastfeed or bottle-feed your baby every 2-3 hours during the day and every 3-4

hours at night.

- **Offer a variety of healthy foods:** Once your baby starts eating solids, offer them a variety of nutritious foods from all the food groups. Let them explore different textures and flavors at their own pace.

- **Take a parenting class:** These classes can provide valuable information on child development and common challenges, and offer a chance to connect with other parents.

- **Join a support group:** Connecting with other parents who are going through similar experiences can be a great source of support and encouragement.

"

"The two most important things I give my children are roots and wings."

- HODDING CARTER

(An American journalist and author)

Part 3:

Empowering the Curious Climber: Your Toddler Years

Inside This Part

Hold on tight! Get ready for the exhilarating ride of toddlerhood. This incredible stage is filled with boundless energy, a thirst for exploration, and a constant desire to learn and grow. But alongside the joy and laughter, there can be tantrums, tears, and moments of frustration. Don't worry, you're not alone!

In this part, we'll equip you with the tools and knowledge you need to navigate these exciting (and sometimes challenging) toddler years. Here's a sneak peek at what awaits you:

- **Understanding Their Development:** We'll delve into the fascinating world of toddler development, exploring the incredible milestones your little one will achieve – physically, cognitively, and emotionally.
- **The Power of Play:** Get ready to unlock the magic of play in your toddler's learning journey! We'll show you how simple activities can spark curiosity, ignite creativity, and foster important skills..
- **Promoting Positive Communication:** Learn the power of positive communication with your toddler. We'll show you how to navigate even the trickiest situations with empathy, understanding, and the right words.
- **Conquering Everyday Hurdles:** Tantrums, separation anxiety, and sleep issues – we've all been there! We'll equip you with practical solutions to overcome these common challenges, promoting a calmer and more peaceful home life.

So, get ready to embrace the wonder of toddlerhood! With the tools and knowledge in this section, you'll be well-equipped to guide your little explorer on their incredible journey of growth and discovery.

Understanding Their Development: The Wonderful World of Toddlers

You've officially entered the whirlwind adventure that is toddlerhood. Buckle up for a rollercoaster ride filled with boundless energy (think a never-ending battery!), insatiable curiosity, and a constant desire to explore everything within reach. It's a stage of incredible growth, both physically and mentally, and while there will be moments of frustration and tear-filled tantrums (we've all been there!), there's also immense joy and laughter to be shared with your little one.

This period, roughly between the ages of one to three, is a time of rapid development. You'll witness your child blossoming before your eyes, mastering new skills seemingly overnight. One day they'll be taking those first wobbly steps, the next they'll be climbing furniture with surprising agility (cue the heart palpitations!). Their language skills will explode, from babbling and one-word utterances to forming simple sentences and expressing their wants and needs. You might even be surprised by their newfound independence – that once clingy baby is now determined to do things on their own, from putting on shoes (even if they end up on the wrong feet) to attempting to feed themselves.

It's important to remember that every child develops at their own pace. There will be milestones you eagerly await, like their first word or those independent steps, but don't get discouraged if they don't happen exactly when the books say they should. Focus on celebrating their unique journey and the amazing things they're accomplishing every day.

As parents, you play a vital role in fostering this development. Your love, support, and guidance will be the foundation for their emotional well-being and future success. By providing a safe and stimulating environment filled with opportunities for exploration and play, you'll be nurturing their curiosity and helping them discover the world around them. This section will equip you with the knowledge and tools you need to navigate this exciting stage, from understanding their developmental leaps to navigating those inevitable tantrums. We'll delve into the importance of play, explore strategies for building emotional intelligence, and offer practical tips for establishing healthy boundaries and fostering positive communication.

During this stage, you might find yourself picking up more toys than laundry (and that's okay!). It's a time of boundless energy and exploration, and sometimes that exploration involves emptying an entire container of cereal onto the floor (cue the laughter, and maybe the vacuum cleaner). But trust us, amidst the mess and the occasional tantrum, there's magic in watching your little one discover the world around them.

Sensory play is a fantastic way to nurture this curiosity. Providing opportunities for your toddler to explore different textures, sounds, and smells can stimulate their learning and growth. From squishy play dough to building block towers, the possibilities are endless!

It's also important to remember that every toddler is unique. Some might be more cautious and take their time exploring new things, while others dive headfirst into adventure. There's no "right" way to be a toddler, and all these variations are perfectly normal. As parents, you can learn more about different temperaments and find resources to help you understand your little one's unique personality.

Finally, don't underestimate the power of observation. Watch how your toddler interacts with the world, what sparks their curiosity, and what activities they gravitate towards. Following their lead and incorporating their interests into playtime routines can create a fun and stimulating learning environment.

Witnessing your child's incredible growth during the toddler years is a symphony of joy, discovery, and yes, sometimes a few messy mishaps (remember the cereal incident?). But with this rapid development comes new challenges. How do you navigate those epic tantrums? How do you establish boundaries while fostering their independence? How do you help them understand and express their emotions in healthy ways?

In the next section, we'll delve deeper into these questions and equip you with the tools you need to navigate this exciting, and sometimes messy, stage. We'll explore the power of play in fostering your toddler's development, discover strategies for building their emotional intelligence, and offer practical tips for working together to create a happy and harmonious home. So, take a deep breath, embrace the chaos, and get ready to unlock the secrets of the "terrible twos" (spoiler alert: they're not always so terrible!).

In Action: Quiet Time and Play Dates 

✓ **The Party Animal:** David, an introvert, found himself drained by his son Noah's boundless social energy. Noah, a vibrant three-year-old, transformed the house into his personal stage, demanding constant attention. David craved quiet time but knew he couldn't shield Noah from the world.

He incorporated "quiet time" activities and enrolled Noah in a music class, finding a balance that worked for both. During park visits, David wouldn't shut Noah down but politely introduced him to other kids. Noah thrived, and David learned to navigate his son's personality while respecting his own boundaries.

Make it Happen: Tips for Your Toddler's Routine 

✓ Level Up Your Parenthood:
  - Create a safe play space for your toddler: This could be a designated area in your living room with age-appropriate toys and activities.
  - Develop a consistent routine for your toddler: This includes mealtimes, nap times, and bedtime.
  - Provide opportunities for sensory play: This could include activities like playing with play dough, building

block towers, or finger painting.
- **Enroll your toddler in a playgroup or daycare:** This can help them socialize with other children.

The Power of Play:
Activities for Learning and Growth

Remember those days filled with diaper changes, feeding schedules, and precious gurgles? Now, your little explorer is on the move, their curiosity blossoming like a flower reaching for the sun. This burst of exploration and discovery, roughly between the ages of one and three, is fueled by the incredible power of play.

Think of play as your child's own learning lab. Through open-ended activities and imaginative adventures, they're developing essential life skills. From building block towers that reach for the ceiling to creating mud pies in the backyard, every playful moment is a stepping stone towards cognitive development, emotional intelligence, and social skills. Here's how you can turn everyday moments into magical learning experiences:

- **Sensory Explosion:** Toddlers are fascinated by the world around them. Engage their senses by filling a bin with dry beans or rice for them to explore. Offer colorful scarves for twirling, or create a homemade play dough batch for them to mold.

- **Creative Coloring Capers:** Coloring books aren't just for keeping little hands busy – they're a wonderful tool for sparking creativity and developing fine motor skills. Explore coloring books with bold illustrations and chunky shapes perfect for little hands. Let your child experiment with colors and encourage them to tell you a story about their creation. Sticker books take creativity a step further. Look for reusable sticker books with themes like animals, vehicles, or clothing. Your child can create scenes and stories by placing and replacing the stickers and practicing hand-eye coordination and spatial reasoning along the way.

- **Block Party:** Building block towers is not just a simple activity. It's a powerhouse for cognitive development, encouraging spatial reasoning, problem-solving, and hand-eye coordination. Blocks also provide a blank canvas for imaginative play. One moment your living room can be a towering castle, the next a bustling city block – all fueled by your child's creativity.

- **Story Time Shenanigans:** Reading stories together isn't just about language skills. It's a wonderful opportunity to bond and introduce new concepts and emotions. Bring the stories to life with silly voices, act out the characters, or encourage your child to create their own endings.

- **The Great Outdoors:** There's a whole world waiting to be explored right outside your doorstep! Head to the park for a picnic, take a nature walk to collect leaves, or simply splash in puddles after a rain shower. The fresh air and open space will do wonders for your child's physical and mental well-being, while the natural world provides endless opportunities for exploration and learning.

The Benefits of Play

Imagine your child's world as a giant, interactive learning lab. Every playful moment, from meticulously stacking blocks to brewing pretend tea, contributes to their overall development.

Play acts as the fuel for a blossoming mind. Through exploration and experimentation, they build critical thinking skills. Stacking colorful blocks teaches them about spatial relationships, while pretend play becomes a springboard for their imagination.

But play isn't just about building castles. It's also a fantastic way for your child to develop social and emotional skills. Playtime becomes a safe space where they learn valuable lessons about cooperation and sharing. Play can also be a healthy outlet for expressing emotions. Sometimes, building a towering block masterpiece represents pride. Other times, a dramatic meltdown during a pretend tea party might be their way of expressing frustration.

Don't forget the physical benefits of play! Running around, jumping in puddles, or climbing on furniture (with supervision!) – all these playful activities help develop gross motor skills like balance and coordination. But play also plays a role in refining fine motor skills, those intricate movements that allow them to grasp small objects or manipulate play dough.

Finally, playtime is a constant conversation for your child. As they interact with toys, explore their surroundings, and engage in imaginative scenarios, they're constantly learning new words. Each playful interaction is an opportunity to practice communication skills and develop a love for language.

Making Playtime Magical

The most important ingredient in playtime is you! Get down on the floor and build that block tower together. Sing silly songs and chase bubbles. By being fully present and engaged in your child's world of play, you're not just having fun; you're fostering a love of learning, building a strong bond, and setting them up for success in the years to come.

Play is more than just a fun way to pass the time. It's the foundation for your child's development, shaping their cognitive skills, emotional intelligence, social abilities, and even physical well-being. By embracing the power of play and creating a stimulating and nurturing environment, you're equipping your little one with the tools they need to thrive in the years to come.

This is just the beginning of their incredible adventure. As you navigate the "terrible twos" and witness their blossoming independence in the coming sections, you'll discover even more ways to use the power of play to nurture their growth and development. Here are some additional tips to make playtime enriching and enjoyable for everyone:

- **The Importance of Open-Ended Toys:** While specific-purpose toys are great, consider incorporating more open-ended toys like building blocks, nesting cups, play dough, wooden blocks, or even cardboard boxes! These spark creativity and imagination.

- **Embrace the Mess:** We know, a scattered living room or a mud-filled backyard might not be ideal. But here's the secret: a little disorder is a sign of great learning happening! Embrace the mess (within reason, of course!), and focus on the joy of exploration.

- **Let Your Child Lead the Way:** Playtime is a fantastic opportunity to observe your child's interests and developmental needs. Instead of dictating every activity, watch what sparks their curiosity and follow their lead. This could involve building a tower out of blocks, creating a pretend grocery store with empty food containers, or putting on a puppet show with stuffed animals. By allowing them to take charge, you're nurturing their autonomy and fostering a love of independent exploration.

- **Playtime for All Ages:** Play isn't just for toddlers! As your child grows, continue to incorporate playtime into your routines, adapting the activities to their age and interests. Board games, building elaborate Lego creations, or even having a family dance party are all fantastic ways to bond, have fun, and keep the spirit of play alive throughout their childhood.

As you've seen, playtime isn't just about fun and giggles (although there are plenty of those too!). It's the foundation for so many essential skills your little one is developing. But the world of toddlers isn't just sunshine and rainbows. There will be meltdowns, tears, and moments where you might wonder what emotion your little one is experiencing.

In this next section, we'll delve into the world of emotional intelligence, helping you understand your child's feelings and equip them with the tools to express themselves in healthy ways. We'll explore how to navigate tantrums, validate their emotions, and create a safe space for open communication. So, take a deep breath, and remember, you've got this!

In Action: The Power of Play

✓ **The Budding Artist:** Isabelle, a bright and curious toddler, seemed to have an endless supply of energy. Her imagination constantly amazed her parents, David and Emily. Isabelle turned everything into an opportunity for play – a cardboard box became a spaceship, a pile of pillows, a mountain to climb. While David and Emily appreciated Isabelle's creativity, they worried about the constant mess. A friend suggested introducing open-ended toys. They replaced some of Isabelle's structured toys with building blocks, play dough, and finger paints. Isabelle embraced the new materials, creating elaborate sculptures and masterpieces on large sheets of paper spread on the floor. The open-ended nature of the toys fueled her creativity, and the designated art space contained the mess, making playtime more enjoyable for everyone.

✓ **The Shy Explorer:** Noah, a cautious toddler, preferred the comfort of his favorite stuffed animal over venturing into new experiences. Playdates with other children often ended in tears, as Noah clung to his parents' legs, overwhelmed by the noise and activity. Noah's parents wanted him to develop his social skills but struggled to find ways to encourage him to interact with others. A parenting class offered some valuable insights. The instructor suggested creating a safe and familiar environment for playdates. Noah's parents started inviting one child at a time, allowing Noah to warm up gradually in his own space. They also incorporated familiar toys and activities during playdates, helping Noah feel more comfortable. Over time, Noah began to venture out of his shell, engaging in simple interactions with the other children.

Mindful Parenting: Decoding Playtime Routine 

✓ **Pause & Reflect:**

- Describe a recent playtime experience with your toddler. What did you do, and how did your child respond?
- What are your child's favorite toys and activities?
- How can you create a more stimulating and engaging play space for your toddler at home?
- Think about a time when you struggled to keep playtime positive. What happened, and how did you cope?

Building Emotional Intelligence: Recognizing and Expressing Feelings

Remember when your cuddly newborn responded with a blissful gurgle? Fast forward a year or two, and that same little one might unleash a full-blown tantrum, leaving you wondering what's going on beneath the surface. This spectrum of emotions, from joy to frustration, is all part of your child's development, and helping them navigate this inner world is where emotional intelligence comes in.

Emotional intelligence is like a superpower that allows your child to understand their own feelings and those of others. It's about identifying anger, sadness, or excitement, and expressing them in healthy ways. We play a crucial role in nurturing this superpower.

Everyday Moments as Learning Opportunities

Everyday moments become opportunities to build emotional intelligence. Imagine building a block tower with your child. It's a collaborative effort, filled with giggles, but suddenly the tower crashes, and tears flow. This is a chance to connect: "Oh no, the tower fell down. It looks like you're feeling frustrated. Would you like to help me rebuild it?" By acknowledging their feelings and offering support, you're helping them understand that frustration is normal and there are healthy ways to deal with it.

Examples Across Age Groups:

Strategies for identifying and expressing emotions will evolve as your child grows. Here are some examples for different age groups:

- **Younger Toddlers (1-2 years old):** Focus on simple words and nonverbal cues.
  - **Scenario 1:** Your toddler points to a picture book and whines. **Your Response:** "You're pointing at the book and whining. Let's see, is this the book you wanted to read? Here you go!"
  - **Scenario 2:** Your toddler sees a dog barking on a walk and starts to cry. **Your Response:** "You're crying and pointing at the dog. Are you feeling scared? The doggy is just saying hello. How about we walk on the other side of the street?"
  - **Scenario 3:** Your toddler throws a piece of food on the floor during mealtime. **Your Response:** "Uh oh, the food is on the floor. It looks like you're done eating. Let's clean it up together."
  - **Scenario 4:** Your toddler reaches for a toy on a high shelf and gets frustrated. **Your Response:** "I see you're reaching for the toy, but it's too high. Can I help you get it?"
- **Older Toddlers (2-3 years old):** Introduce more complex vocabulary and encourage them to describe their feelings in more detail.
  - **Scenario 1:** Your child loses a game and starts to pout. Your Response: "It looks like you're feeling sad because you didn't win

the game. Winning is fun, but sometimes we lose too. Is there another game you'd like to play?"

- o **Scenario 2:** Your child sees another child playing with a desired toy and starts whining. Your Response: "You seem frustrated because you want to play with that toy. Maybe we can take turns after they're done?"
- o **Scenario 3:** You tell your child it's time to leave the park, and they throw a tantrum. Your Response: "I know you want to stay at the park, and you're feeling upset about leaving. We can come back tomorrow, but for now, it's time to go home."
- o **Scenario 4:** Your child struggles to put on their shoes and gets discouraged. Your Response: "Putting on shoes can be tricky sometimes. It looks like you're feeling frustrated. Do you want me to help you?"

As you can see, these are just a few examples, and the situations you encounter will vary. The key is to be patient and use these interactions as opportunities to help your child identify and express their emotions in healthy ways.

Building Blocks of Emotional Intelligence

Building emotional intelligence is a journey. Celebrate their victories, no matter how small. Did they use words to express their anger instead of throwing a toy? Give them a high five and let them know you're proud! The more you create a safe space for them to explore their emotions and express themselves freely, the stronger their emotional intelligence will become, equipping them to navigate the complexities of life, build strong relationships, and become confident, resilient individuals.

Our children are constantly learning from us. By openly expressing our emotions in healthy ways, we can show them it's okay to feel happy, sad, frustrated, or scared – and that there are healthy ways to deal with these feelings. There will be days when you might feel like a detective trying to decipher your little one's cryptic cries but remember, even small victories are worth celebrating.

This strong foundation of emotional intelligence will serve them well as they navigate friendships, social situations, and the complexities of growing up. As they enter the preschool years, you'll see this emotional intelligence blossom further as they learn to cooperate, empathize, and resolve conflicts with their peers.

As your little one explores their emotions, you'll also notice a growing sense of independence. They'll want to climb, explore, and make their own choices – which is fantastic! But with this newfound freedom comes the need for clear boundaries, which we'll explore in the next section. Setting boundaries isn't about stifling your child's spirit; it's about creating a framework that helps them feel secure and supported as they explore the world around them. So, take a deep breath, and let's embark on this next exciting chapter together!

In Action: Nurturing Tiny Emotions

- ✓ **The Frustrated Builder:** Liam, a spirited two-year-old, loved building block towers with his dad, Michael. One afternoon, Liam was meticulously constructing a tower when suddenly, with a loud crash, it tumbled to the floor. Liam's face crumpled, and a tear rolled down his cheek. Michael, understanding Liam's frustration, knelt down to his eye level. "Oh no," he said gently, "the tower fell down. It looks like you're feeling frustrated. Would you like to help me rebuild it?" Liam, sniffling slightly, nodded. Together, they rebuilt the tower, taking turns placing blocks and celebrating each successful level. Michael narrated their actions, saying things like, "We're working together as a team!" By acknowledging Liam's feelings and offering comfort and support, Michael helped Liam understand and cope with his frustration in a healthy way.

The Sad Friend: Emma, a curious toddler, loved playing with her friend Chloe at daycare. One day, Chloe arrived with a bandaged arm, unable to play with her usual enthusiasm. Emma, confused by Chloe's lack of energy, started whining. The daycare teacher, Sarah, saw an opportunity to teach about empathy. She crouched down between the two girls and gently explained, "Chloe hurt her arm and isn't feeling well today. Maybe we can offer to help her color a picture?" Emma, considering this, nodded slowly. Sarah provided crayons and paper, and the two girls sat together, coloring pictures while Chloe watched happily. By helping Emma recognize Chloe's feelings and offering an alternative way to play, Sarah planted the seeds of empathy and emotional intelligence.

Make it Happen: Unlocking Your Toddler's Emotions 

✓ Level Up Your Parenthood:
  - Label your child's emotions: Help them understand their feelings by narrating what you see. For example, "I see you're frowning. Are you feeling frustrated?"

- **Validate their feelings:** Let your child know that their feelings are okay. It's OK to feel sad, angry, or frustrated sometimes.
- **Offer comfort and support:** Let your child know you're there for them and help them find healthy ways to express emotions.
- **Model healthy ways to express emotions:** Show your child that it's okay to feel sad or angry, but there are healthy ways to express those feelings, such as talking about them or taking deep breaths.

The Great Balancing Act: *Setting Boundaries with Your Little Explorer*

As your little explorer begins to toddle, climb, and assert their independence, you'll enter a new phase of parenting: setting boundaries. It's a shift from simply reacting to your child's needs to proactively guiding their behavior. Picture it as building a fence around a playground – not to confine them, but to create a safe space where they can play and grow.

Toddlers are like little scientists, constantly testing the limits of their world. They might throw food on the floor, try to climb on the counter, or refuse to brush their teeth. It's not defiance; it's their way of learning cause and effect, understanding what's acceptable, and developing self-control. Their boundless curiosity and strong urge to explore can lead them into trouble, which is where redirection comes in handy. If your little one is making a beeline for that antique vase, a gentle "Let's go build a fort with your pillows instead!" can often divert their attention and prevent a potential disaster.

But where do you, as parents, fit into this picture? Setting boundaries doesn't mean being a drill sergeant; it's about gentle guidance and consistency. Start by observing your child's behavior. What are their triggers? When do meltdowns typically occur? This will help you anticipate potential challenges and set realistic expectations. If you notice your toddler tends to get fussy in the late afternoon, perhaps schedule errands for earlier in the day or plan a quiet activity at home during that time.

Your child's brain is still developing. They don't have the same capacity for reasoning as adults. Instead of lengthy explanations, use simple, clear language. "We use gentle hands with our friends," or "We eat our food at the table." Consistency is key. If you say "no" to climbing on the furniture today, stick to it tomorrow. If you waver, your child will quickly learn that pushing boundaries can be a way to get what they want.

Here's the surprising thing about consistency: When you establish clear routines and expectations, like always eating at the table, you'll often find your little one following suit without a fuss. They crave predictability and will start to anticipate mealtimes by climbing into their highchair on their own. This doesn't mean there won't be occasional resistance, but consistent boundaries will make it easier for them to understand and follow the rules.

This doesn't mean you have to be rigid. There's room for flexibility within boundaries. If your child insists on wearing their superhero costume to the grocery store, let them! It's a harmless way for them to express themselves. But if they refuse to hold your hand while crossing the street, that's a non-negotiable safety issue. Here are some additional ways to offer choices within boundaries:

- **Clothing:** Instead of asking, "Do you want to wear a sweater?" which can be easily declined, offer two choices that fit the weather. "Is it the red or blue sweater you'd like to wear today?"
- **Snack Time:** Provide healthy options but allow them some control. "Would you like carrot sticks or apple slices for your snack?"
- **Bedtime Routine:** Give limited choices within the established routine. "Do you want to brush your teeth before or after you put on your pajamas?"

By offering limited choices, you give your child a sense of control and encourage cooperation. Remember, the key is to provide options that all fulfill your overall goal (getting dressed appropriately, having a healthy snack, following a bedtime routine). You're their role model, so show them how it's done. If you lose your cool, take a deep breath and model how to calm down. Your little one is watching and learning.

Don't forget the power of positive reinforcement and humor. When your child follows the rules, shower them with praise and affection. A heartfelt "You did such a great job sharing your toys!" can go a long way. If things get tense, try injecting humor. Turn putting on shoes into a race or have a silly conversation with their teddy bear. A good laugh can often turn a tantrum around.

But what about those inevitable tantrums? They're a normal part of toddlerhood, a way for your little one to express their frustration when they haven't yet mastered the art of emotional regulation. Stay calm, empathize with their feelings ("I know you're upset, but we can't throw toys"), and offer alternatives ("We can build a block tower instead"). If your child is having a meltdown in a public place, don't be afraid to remove them from the situation to a quieter spot where they can calm down. Sometimes, a natural consequence is the best teacher. If they refuse to wear their jacket, they might get cold and realize why you insisted. Just be sure to use your judgment and always prioritize safety.

Every toddler is unique. Some are more strong-willed than others, while some are more sensitive. Be adaptable and tailor your approach to your child's personality. What works for one child might not work for another. The most important thing is to be consistent, patient, and loving.

Setting boundaries isn't always easy. You might face resistance, tantrums, and days when it feels like you're taking one step forward and two steps back. But remember, you're not just shaping your child's behavior; you're shaping their character, their sense of self, and their understanding of the world around them. Every boundary you set is a building block in their development, a lesson in self-control, respect, and communication.

And speaking of communication, it's the glue that holds everything together. The way you talk to your toddler, the words you choose, and the tone you use, all have a profound impact on their understanding of themselves and the world. In the next section, we'll delve into the art of promoting positive communication, exploring how to empower your little one with words, create a safe space for expression, and navigate those inevitable communication breakdowns with grace and empathy. Because, as you'll soon discover, words matter—they have the power to build bridges, heal wounds, and nurture a lifelong bond of love and understanding.

In Action: The Importance of Clear Boundaries

- ✓ **The Energetic Climber:** Anna, a bright and energetic toddler, loved to explore her surroundings. This sense of adventure often led her to climb on furniture, much to the dismay of her parents, David and Lisa. David and Lisa wanted to encourage Anna's curiosity but also worried about her safety.

  They decided to set clear boundaries around climbing. They gently but firmly explained that climbing on furniture wasn't allowed and offered alternatives like climbing toys or playing on a designated play mat. Anna, initially resistant, gradually understood the rules. David and Lisa provided positive reinforcement when Anna played safely, praising her for her good choices. This consistent approach helped Anna understand boundaries and feel safe in her environment.

- ✓ **The Fussy Eater:** Noah, a picky eater, often turned mealtimes into a battleground. His parents, Mia and Ethan, were at a loss about how to handle his food refusal. They decided to implement a few boundaries around mealtimes. They offered Noah a choice of two healthy options, but dessert was not negotiable unless he ate his dinner first. Mia and Ethan also avoided distractions like television during meals, focusing on creating a calm and enjoyable mealtime experience. There were occasions when Noah threw a tantrum, but Mia and Ethan stayed calm, repeated the expectations, and offered him quiet time until he was ready to try his food again. Over time, Noah became more receptive to trying new foods and understanding the boundaries around mealtimes.

Promoting Positive Communication: *Words Matter*

Remember those early days of cooing and babbling? Your little one has come a long way since. Now, they're a vibrant burst of words, opinions, and questions. Their vocabulary might still be a work in progress, but their ability to communicate their needs, desires, and emotions is rapidly expanding. This is a crucial time for you, as parents, to lay the groundwork for strong and lasting communication.

As parents, we have the incredible opportunity to shape and nurture this budding communication style. We can teach our toddlers how to express themselves effectively, listen with empathy, and resolve conflicts peacefully. We can help them understand that words are powerful tools that can build bridges, mend fences, and create lasting connections.

It all starts with the words we choose. Think of your toddler as a sponge, soaking up every word, tone, and inflection you use. Here are some everyday examples of how to promote positive communication, broken down by age group:

12-18 Months:
- **Simple Explanations:** Narrate your actions as you go about your day. "I'm putting away the toys now. It's time for lunch!" This helps them connect words with actions and build their understanding of language.
- **Positive Reinforcement:** Instead of saying "No don't touch," use positive redirection: "Gentle hands with the cup, please." This teaches them appropriate behavior and the concept of gentleness.
- **Labeling Emotions:** Help them identify their feelings. "Are you feeling frustrated because you can't reach that toy? Let's try together."

18-24 Months:
- **Open-Ended Questions:** Instead of yes or no questions, use open-ended prompts to encourage conversation: "What color is your block?" or "What do you want to play with next?"

- **Active Listening:** Pay attention when they speak, make eye contact, and respond with simple phrases like "Uh-huh" or "I see." This shows them their words have value and encourages them to keep talking. For example, if they're pointing at the door, you could say, "You want to go outside? Let's see if we can find your shoes!"
- **Choices:** Offer limited choices to give them a sense of control: "Do you want to wear the red or blue shirt today?"

2-3 Years Old:
- **Storytelling:** Read books together and discuss the characters' feelings and actions. "How do you think the puppy feels when he loses his bone?" This helps them develop empathy and understand different perspectives.
- **"I" Statements:** Model using "I" statements to express your feelings: "I feel frustrated when you throw your toys. Can we put them away together?" This teaches them a healthy way to communicate their emotions.
- **Take Turns:** Practice turn-taking during conversations. This teaches them patience and the importance of listening to others.

By following these tips, you can help your child develop strong communication skills that will benefit them throughout their lives.

Another important aspect of positive communication is active listening and nonverbal cues. When your toddler is talking, get down on their level, make eye contact, and give them your full attention. A warm smile, a gentle touch, or a reassuring hug can speak volumes. Your toddler is constantly watching you, absorbing your facial expressions, body language, and tone of voice. By modeling calm and positive communication, even when you're feeling stressed, you're teaching them invaluable lessons about emotional regulation and conflict resolution.

And don't underestimate the power of nonverbal communication. A warm smile, a gentle touch, or a reassuring hug can speak volumes. Sometimes, the most effective way to communicate is through simple gestures of love and understanding. Your toddler is constantly watching you, absorbing your facial expressions, body language, and tone of voice. By modeling calm and positive communication, even when you're feeling stressed, you're teaching them invaluable lessons about emotional regulation and conflict resolution. After all, actions often speak louder than words.

Instead, focus on their efforts and progress, no matter how small. Celebrate their victories, acknowledge their struggles, and let them know you believe in them. Each interaction is an opportunity to build a stronger connection and equip your child with the tools they need to navigate the world with confidence and compassion.

Positive communication isn't just about what you say; it's also about what you don't say. Avoid labeling your child ("You're being naughty") or comparing them to others ("Why can't you be more like your sister?"). These words can be deeply hurtful and chip away at their self-esteem. Instead, focus on their efforts and progress, no matter how small. Celebrate their victories, acknowledge their struggles, and let them know you believe in them. Each interaction is an opportunity to build a stronger connection and equip your child with the tools they need to navigate the world with confidence and compassion.

Now, let's face it: even with the most effective communication strategies in place, there will be moments when your toddler's emotions erupt like a volcano, when separation anxiety rears its head, or when sleep seems like a distant dream. But fear not, dear parents. In the next section, we'll dive into these "everyday hurdles" with practical tips, gentle guidance, and a sprinkle of humor to help you navigate the choppy waters of toddlerhood with resilience and grace.

In Action: Building Little Communicators

✓ **The Selective Listener:** Noah, a spirited three-year-old, had his own mind. Mealtimes were a constant battleground. His parents, David and Lisa, often felt like they were talking to a brick wall when they tried to persuade him to eat his vegetables. David and Lisa decided to revamp their mealtime communication strategy. They started by offering Noah choices within healthy boundaries. For example, they might say, "Would you like broccoli or carrots with your dinner tonight?" They also incorporated open-ended questions like, "What color is your favorite veggie?" to spark conversation about healthy foods. Finally, they focused on positive reinforcement, praising Noah for trying new bites and celebrating his willingness to participate in mealtime conversations. Gradually, Noah became more receptive to trying new foods and engaged more during mealtimes. By incorporating choices, open-ended questions, and positive reinforcement, David and Lisa helped Noah develop better listening skills and a more positive association with mealtimes.

✓ **The Chatty Car Ride:** Maya, a talkative three-year-old, often turned car rides into lively chats. Her mom, Emily, appreciated Maya's enthusiasm but sometimes felt overwhelmed during long errands. Emily decided to incorporate open-ended questions and storytelling into their car rides. She would ask questions like, "What color are the cars we see?" or tell stories about imaginary characters like a friendly bus that helped people get to work. This engaged Maya, encouraged conversation, and made car rides more enjoyable for both of them. By using open-ended questions and storytelling, Emily promoted positive communication and created a more engaging experience for Maya.

Make it Happen: Talk Time Tools 

✓ Level Up Your Parenthood:
- **Practice active listening**: When your child talks, get down on their level, make eye contact, and give them your full attention.
- **Use positive reinforcement**: Praise your child's efforts to communicate and express themselves clearly.
- **Model appropriate communication**: Show your child how to use "I" statements, and take turns talking.
- **Narrate your day**: Talk about what you're doing throughout the day to help your child connect words with actions and build their understanding of language.
- **Read together**: Reading books together exposes your child to new vocabulary and opens up discussions about characters' feelings and actions.
- **Limit screen time**: Excessive screen time can hinder language development.
- **Be patient and consistent**: It takes time and practice for toddlers to develop strong communication skills.

Conquering Everyday Hurdles: Tantrums, Separation Anxiety, Sleep Issues, The Potty Training

If you're reading this, chances are you've experienced a few (or more than a few) of those classic toddler hurdles: the ear-splitting tantrums, the clinginess that rivals a koala bear, the sleep deprivation that makes you question whether caffeine is a food group, and let's not forget, the potty training roller coaster. But fear not, you're not alone! This section is your survival guide, packed with practical tips, gentle guidance, and a sprinkle of humor to help you navigate the choppy waters of toddlerhood with resilience and grace.

Let's be real, parents. There will be days when it feels like your toddler's vocabulary consists solely of the word "no," accompanied by a soundtrack of ear-piercing shrieks and dramatic floor drops. These are the days when tantrums reign supreme, leaving you questioning your sanity and wondering if you'll ever make it out of the grocery store without a scene.

While tantrums can erupt anywhere, they are especially common during outings like shopping trips. Here are some tips to avoid meltdowns before they start:

- **Manage expectations:** Talk to your toddler about the purpose of the trip. Explain where you're going and what you'll be doing. If you won't be buying toys, let them know beforehand.
- **Time it right:** Don't schedule errands when your toddler is tired or hungry. A well-rested and fed little one is a calmer little one.
- **Pack distractions:** Bring a favorite toy, a healthy snack, or a busy bag with crayons and coloring books to keep them occupied.
- **Limit screen time:** Avoid screens in the car or right before leaving the house. Returning to reality can trigger frustration.
- **Embrace Choice:** When possible, offer your toddler small choices to give them a sense of control. Let them pick their outfit (within limits), or choose between two healthy snacks.

Tantrums can be triggered by various factors: hunger, fatigue, overstimulation, a change in routine, or simply not getting what they want. It's like a tiny storm raging within them, and it needs to run its course. However, understanding the triggers can help you anticipate and possibly prevent some meltdowns. If you know your child gets cranky when they're hungry, offer a snack before heading out. If they're easily overwhelmed, avoid overly stimulating environments or plan breaks in quiet areas. Even with planning, tantrums can happen. Here's what to do when they erupt:

- **Stay Calm:** Your calmness will help regulate your child's emotions. Take a deep breath and project a soothing demeanor.
- **Acknowledge Feelings:** Say things like "I see you're upset" or "It's

okay to feel frustrated." This validates their emotions.

- **Distraction is Your Friend:** If your toddler starts eyeing something they want, distract them with a game of "I Spy" or point out something interesting in another part of the store (or park, or wherever you are).
- **Be Clear and Consistent:** If a tantrum hits over a desired item, use simple, firm language to explain it's not on the agenda or within budget. Avoid lengthy discussions or bargaining.
- **"It's Not Ours" Approach - Rethink It:** While there's nothing wrong with explaining something isn't yours until you buy it, this approach might not be effective for toddlers. Toddlers are still grasping object permanence, and saying "It's not yours" might make them think the desired item has disappeared, leading to frustration. Instead, explain you'll see if you can get them the item "next time" or after completing errands.

Sometimes, a change of scenery can work wonders. If you're at home, guide your child to their "calm-down corner" – a cozy space with soft pillows, books, and maybe a favorite stuffed animal. If you're out in public, don't hesitate to remove your child from the situation to a quieter spot where they can regain their composure. In the heat of the moment, it might feel like the tantrum will last forever, but remember, it will pass. Afterward, take a moment to connect with your child, offer a hug, and talk about what happened. This helps them learn to process their emotions and develop coping skills.

If a tantrum escalates or doesn't seem to end, it's important to remain calm and avoid giving into demands. This can be difficult, but remember, consistency is key. If your child learns that tantrums get them what they want, they're more likely to repeat the behavior. Instead, try offering a simple choice within the boundaries you've set. For example, if they're throwing a fit about leaving the park, you could say, "Would you like to walk to the car or should I carry you?"

Dealing with tantrums in different situations can require different approaches. At home, you have more control over the environment and can easily redirect or offer a calming activity. In a store, you might need to leave your shopping cart and find a quiet corner or even leave the store altogether. In the car, pull over to a safe spot if possible, and offer comfort and reassurance until the tantrum subsides.

Every tantrum is a learning opportunity for both you and your child. With patience, understanding, and a toolbox of strategies, you can help your little one navigate these emotional storms and emerge stronger and more resilient. Tantrums are a normal part of toddler development. By remaining calm and responding with empathy and consistency, you can help your child learn to regulate their emotions and develop healthy coping mechanisms.

Sticky Kisses: When Goodbyes Feel Scary

And there are those sticky kisses! It's that heart-wrenching moment when your little one clings to you like a baby koala, refusing to let go even for a short visit. While it can be difficult to see them upset, remember these sticky kisses are a sign of a special bond. They're your little one's way of saying they feel safe and secure with you, their favorite grown-up. Separation anxiety is a normal developmental stage for toddlers, usually peaking around 18 months. It shows they're starting to understand that people come and go, but it can also be a source of stress for both of you.

To ease the transition, establish consistent routines, create comforting rituals (like a special goodbye song or a stuffed animal to hold), and gradually increase the time you spend apart. Most importantly, reassure your child that you'll always come back. Here's the key: When making promises about pick-up times, be very specific and stick to it as much as possible. Little ones often take things very literally. If you tell them you'll pick them up "after lunch," that timeframe might be meaningless to them. Instead, try saying, "I'll be back to get you at 1:00 pm, right after story time." This concrete information helps them visualize when they can expect to see you again, reducing anxiety.

Of course, unforeseen circumstances can arise. But whenever possible, do your best to be on time for pick-up. If something unavoidable delays you, call the caregiver and explain the situation to both them and your child. Briefly explain that you'll be a bit later than planned, but be sure to give a new, specific pick-up time. This helps maintain trust and prevents them from feeling abandoned.

When it comes to saying goodbye, keep it short and sweet. Lingering can make it difficult for your child to adjust. And don't sneak away when they're not looking; this can erode trust. Instead, say a loving goodbye and reassure them that you'll see them soon. You can even set up a special "goodbye" ritual, like a secret handshake or a special phrase you say together.

Sleep Struggles: Recharging Your Toddler (and You!)

Sleep, or rather, the lack thereof, is a familiar foe for many parents of toddlers. While newborns might have kept you up with frequent feedings, toddlers present a new set of sleep challenges. Bedtime battles, nighttime wakings, and early mornings can leave you feeling like a zombie. But take heart, there are strategies to regain those precious hours of rest for both you and your little one.

First, let's revisit the basics. Unlike newborns who sleep in short bursts throughout the day and night, toddlers typically need 11 to 14 hours of sleep in a 24-hour period, including naps. This amount of sleep is crucial for their physical and mental development, supporting everything from growth hormone production to memory consolidation.

Establishing a consistent bedtime routine is key. Aim for a bedtime between 6:30 pm and 8:30 pm and a consistent wake-up time, even on weekends. Consistency is key, but don't stress about late nights on occasional weekends. A consistent wake-up time, even on weekends, can help regulate your child's internal clock and promote better sleep quality. Dimming the lights an hour before bed, reading calming stories, and offering a warm bath can all signal to your toddler that it's time to wind down.

A calm and cozy sleep environment is also essential. Make sure your child's room is dark, quiet, and cool. Consider using blackout curtains to block out any light, a white noise machine to mask distracting sounds, and a fan or air conditioner to maintain a comfortable temperature.

As for the age-old question of co-sleeping versus separate sleeping, there's no one-size-fits-all answer. Some families find that co-sleeping promotes bonding and makes nighttime parenting easier, while others prefer the independence and uninterrupted sleep that separate sleeping can provide. Ultimately, the choice is yours, and it's important to do what feels right for your family.

If you do choose to co-sleep, be sure to follow safe sleep practices, such as ensuring your child has their own designated sleep space on a firm surface with no loose bedding or pillows. If you opt for separate sleeping, consider starting with a crib in your room and gradually transitioning your child to their own room when they're ready.

Patience is key. Sleep habits can take time to establish, and setbacks are normal. But with consistent effort and a few adjustments, you can help your toddler (and yourself!) get the rest you need to thrive. If sleep problems persist, don't hesitate to talk to your pediatrician for guidance and support.

Besides night sleep, daytime naps are also crucial for toddlers. They provide a much-needed recharge, helping them regulate their emotions, consolidate memories, and stay energized for the rest of the day. Most toddlers need one to two naps per day, but as they get older, they may transition to a single afternoon nap or drop naps altogether.

By prioritizing healthy sleep habits from an early age, you're not only setting your child up for a lifetime of restorative rest, you're also investing in their overall well-being and happiness. A well-rested child is a happy child, and a happy child makes for a happier parent!

The Potty Training Puzzle: Navigating the Ups and Downs

Every parent eagerly awaits the moment their little one conquers the potty training puzzle. But this milestone, while momentous, rarely unfolds like a smooth fairy tale. Each child develops at their own pace, and the journey is likely to be peppered with accidents and setbacks. Here's where your patience, a sprinkle of positive reinforcement, and a healthy dose of humor become your best allies.

Before diving headfirst into the world of potties, take a moment to observe your child. Are they showing signs of readiness? Perhaps they're staying dry for longer stretches or expressing a newfound curiosity about the potty itself. But there are other subtle clues to watch for as well. Does your little one seem increasingly aware of wetness or messiness? Can they follow simple instructions, like walking to the potty when prompted? And most importantly, is there a growing desire for independence peeking through?

If these signs are starting to twinkle like stars in your child's development, it's time to introduce the potty in a fun and positive way. Let your little one choose a special potty seat that speaks to their interests, or transform a plain one into a masterpiece with colorful stickers. Dive into books about potty training adventures and create a soundtrack of silly potty songs to make the whole experience light and engaging. By incorporating these playful elements, you'll be setting the stage for a successful (and hopefully less stressful) potty training journey.

Many parents find success with a gradual approach. Here's how to navigate the transition between diapers and underpants:

- **Start with Pull-Ups (Optional):** If you choose, consider using pull-ups as a stepping stone. They offer a sense of security for your child while still allowing them to feel wetness, a crucial learning step.
- **Underwear During the Day, Diapers at Night:** Once your child shows some progress, dress them in underwear during the day. At night, use diapers until they achieve nighttime dryness. This gradual approach can prevent frustration and accidents.
- **Waterproof Coverings:** Consider using waterproof covers on furniture or car seats to protect against accidents during the learning phase.

Accidents are inevitable during potty training, and that's perfectly okay! Imagine yourself learning a brand new skill - there will be stumbles along the way. The key is to stay calm and reassuring when these mishaps happen. Avoid any temptation to shame or scold your child. Instead, gently remind them that accidents are a normal part of learning, and offer a reassuring hug. Positive reinforcement is your secret weapon! Here are some ways to make using the potty a fun and rewarding experience:

- **The Sticker Celebration:** Create a colorful sticker chart together. Each time your child successfully uses the potty, let them proudly add a sticker to their chart. This visual reminder of their progress will boost their confidence.
- **The Potty Throne Awaits:** Let your child choose a special "potty throne" toy - a small stuffed animal or a favorite action figure - to keep them company during their potty adventures. This little buddy can offer silent encouragement and make potty time feel less intimidating.
- **Big Kid Undies with Super Powers:** Take your child on a shopping trip to pick out some fun and exciting big-kid underwear. Look for designs with their favorite characters or in bright, eye-catching colors. Having these "super-powered" undies can make your child feel more grown-up and excited about using the potty.
- **The Magic Potty Button:** Consider getting a special potty training book with an interactive sound button. When your child uses the potty successfully, they can press the button to hear a celebratory cheer or encouraging song. This interactive element adds a layer of fun and positive reinforcement to the process.

By incorporating these tips and celebrating every success, no matter how small, you'll be creating a positive and supportive environment for your child's potty training journey. Remember, potty training is a process, not a race. There's no need to rush. Follow your child's lead, be patient and supportive, and celebrate every little victory along the way.

From Toddlers to Thrivers: Preparing for Preschool

The toddler years are a dynamic journey of growth, learning, and yes, a few challenges along the way. There's no magic wand to banish tantrums, separation anxiety, sleep disruptions, or potty training mishaps. But by approaching these hurdles with patience, understanding, and a gentle touch, you can transform them into opportunities for connection, growth, and resilience. Embrace the messy, the chaotic, and the beautiful moments, for they are all part of this extraordinary journey called parenthood.

As your child grows and develops, new horizons will open up, new challenges will emerge, and new joys will be discovered. In the next part, we'll venture into the enchanting world of preschool, where imagination reigns supreme, friendships blossom, and a thirst for knowledge takes root. We'll explore how to foster your child's creativity, nurture their social and emotional skills, and prepare them for the exciting adventures that await them in the years ahead. So, let's turn the page and start this next chapter together!

Mindful Parenting: Decoding Playtime Routine 

✓ Pause & Reflect:

- Reflect on a recent time you struggled to communicate effectively with your toddler. What could you have done differently?
- Imagine your child is all grown up. What are three qualities you hope they will possess? How can you nurture those qualities now?
- Describe a time you felt overwhelmed by tantrums or challenging behavior. How did you cope?

66

"The more that you can let go and allow a child to be a child, the more completely he will develop into a healthy, well-rounded person."

- VIRGINIA SATIR

(An American author, clinical social worker, and psychotherapist)

Part 4:

The Superheroes of Imagination: The Preschool Years

Inside This Part

Welcome to the world of preschoolers, where imaginations run wild, friendships blossom, and a thirst for knowledge takes root! As your child enters this exciting new stage, you'll witness a remarkable transformation. They'll go from toddlers who are learning to walk and talk, to little adventurers who are eager to explore the world around them and express themselves in new and creative ways.

Here's a glimpse of what you'll discover in this part:

- **Understanding Your Preschooler's Journey:** Insights into the social, emotional, and cognitive development of preschoolers, along with age-appropriate expectations and milestones.
- **Cultivating Emotional Intelligence:** Guidance on helping your child identify, understand, and express their emotions in healthy ways, and developing empathy for others.
- **Nurturing Your Preschooler's Confidence:** Strategies for fostering a positive self-image, encouraging independence, and building resilience in the face of challenges.
- **Navigating Preschool Challenges:** Practical advice for addressing common concerns like separation anxiety, social conflicts, picky eating, and bedtime struggles.

By the end of this part, you'll be armed with a treasure trove of tools and strategies to champion your preschooler's burgeoning independence, creativity, and zest for learning. Get ready to witness your child transform into a true superhero of imagination, ready to take on the world with a smile and a spark in their eyes. Let's dive in and discover the magic that awaits!

Understanding Your Preschooler's Journey:
Social Development and Beyond

Imagine this: Your once-solitary little one, who used to be perfectly content playing alone with their toys, is now suddenly fascinated by other children. They want to share, take turns, and play make-believe together. Welcome to the preschool years — a time of remarkable social and emotional growth!

As your child's world expands beyond the familiar faces of family, they begin to develop a sense of themselves in relation to others. They begin to understand the concept of friendship, learn how to navigate social interactions and discover the joy of cooperation and collaboration.

It's like watching a tiny superhero in training. Your preschooler is developing their social superpowers:

- **Empathy:** The ability to understand and share the feelings of others, a crucial skill for building strong relationships.
- **Cooperation:** The ability to work together towards a common goal, whether it's building a block tower or playing a game of tag.
- **Conflict Resolution:** The ability to navigate disagreements and find peaceful solutions, a skill that will serve them well throughout their lives.
- **Communication Skills:** The ability to express their thoughts, feelings, and needs clearly and respectfully, and listen attentively to others.

But just like any superhero-in-training, your little one will face challenges along the way. They might struggle with sharing, taking turns, or dealing with disappointment. They might have disagreements with friends or experience social anxiety in new situations. These are all normal parts of the learning process. As their guide, you can help them navigate these challenges with grace and understanding.

In this part, we'll explore the fascinating world of preschool social development. We'll delve into the typical milestones you can expect at different ages, from parallel play (playing alongside others without much interaction) to cooperative play (working together towards a shared goal) to the formation of genuine friendships based on shared interests and mutual trust. We'll also highlight the importance of emotional intelligence in building strong social relationships. We'll share practical strategies for teaching empathy, conflict resolution, and communication skills, such as active listening, using "I" statements to express feelings, and finding win-win solutions to conflicts.

Of course, we won't shy away from the common social challenges that preschoolers face. We'll offer practical tips for dealing with everything from playground disagreements to birthday party meltdowns. For instance, if your child is having trouble sharing, you might suggest taking turns with a toy or setting a timer for each child's turn. If your child is struggling to make friends, you could encourage them to join a playgroup or extracurricular activity where they can meet other children with similar interests.

Every child is unique, and their social development will unfold at its own pace. Celebrate your child's strengths, offer gentle guidance when they stumble, and create a supportive environment where they feel safe to explore, learn, and grow. And as you witness your preschooler blossoming socially and emotionally, you'll also see their imagination ignite. In the next section, we'll delve into the power of play-based learning, uncovering how those seemingly simple games of make-believe, building blocks, and dress-up are actually laying the foundation for your child's future success.

In Action: Social Strides

✓ **The Sharing Struggles:** Ethan, a spirited four-year-old, had a difficult time sharing his toys. Playdates often ended in tears, with Ethan adamantly refusing to share his favorite trucks or action figures. Ethan's parents knew they needed to address his possessive behavior. They started by introducing the concept of taking turns through simple board games and reading stories about sharing and cooperation. They also labeled Ethan's emotions, acknowledging his frustration when he didn't want to share but gently reminding him that sharing is a part of being a good friend. When playdates turned into meltdowns, Ethan's parents introduced a "sharing bin" filled with toys Ethan was comfortable sharing with his friends. This way, Ethan maintained some sense of control while still participating in cooperative play. Over time, with consistent guidance and positive reinforcement, Ethan became more open to sharing. He learned the joy of playing together and the importance of reciprocity in friendships. By implementing clear expectations and offering alternatives, Ethan's parents helped him develop essential social skills like sharing and cooperation.

Make it Happen: Unlocking Your Toddler's Emotions 

✓ **Level Up Your Parenthood:**
- **Enroll Your Child in Playgroups or Activities:** Provide opportunities for your child to interact with other children in a safe and supervised environment.
- **Model Social Skills:** Show your child how to interact with others by using kind words, taking turns, and sharing.
- **Create a "Sharing Bin":** Designate a bin filled with toys your child is comfortable sharing with others during playdates.
- **Celebrate Social Victories:** Acknowledge and praise your child's efforts to share, take turns, or cooperate with others.

The Power of Play-Based Learning: Spark Curiosity and Growth Through Play

Remember those magical days of childhood, when a simple cardboard box transformed into a spaceship, a blanket became a magnificent castle, and a pile of leaves morphed into a dragon's lair? As parents, we can sometimes overlook the immense power of play. It's not just a way to keep kids entertained; it's the cornerstone of a child's development.

Preschool is a critical time for brain development. Play is the primary language children use to learn and explore. Here's a deeper look at the magic behind playtime:

- **Cognitive Development:** Building with blocks isn't just about stacking shapes. It's about mastering concepts like balance, cause-and-effect, and spatial reasoning. Preschoolers develop critical thinking skills as they experiment, troubleshoot, and persevere through challenges while building their creations.

- **Social and Emotional Learning:** Dress-up isn't just about costumes. It's about exploring different identities, developing empathy by pretending to be doctors or caregivers, and practicing communication skills as they interact with their "patients." Imaginative play with friends fosters teamwork, negotiation, and conflict resolution – all essential social and emotional skills.
- **Language Development:** Through play, children create narratives, engage in pretend conversations, and experiment with sounds. Open-ended questions like "What are you building?" or "Tell me about your doctor's visit" encourage them to think creatively and express themselves clearly.
- **Emotional Regulation:** Play provides a safe space for children to explore complex emotions. They can act out anxieties or fears, develop coping mechanisms, and build resilience through pretend scenarios.

In the preschool years, play isn't just about having fun (although that's a huge part of it!). It's the primary way children learn about the world, experiment with different roles, develop social skills and express their creativity. It's their laboratory, their stage, and training ground for life. It's where they get to be messy, silly, and adventurous – all while building essential skills that will equip them well as they navigate their future.

Think about it: When your child builds a tower of blocks, they're not just stacking shapes; they're exploring concepts like balance, gravity, and spatial reasoning. They're learning to plan, problem-solve, and persevere through challenges. When they dress up as a doctor, they're not just trying on clothes; they're experimenting with different identities, practicing empathy, and developing language skills. When they engage in imaginative play with their friends, they're not just having fun; they're learning to cooperate, negotiate, and resolve conflicts. These playful interactions are the building blocks of social and emotional intelligence.

Play is the ultimate brain-builder, stimulating neural connections, enhancing memory and attention, and fostering problem-solving skills. It's also a powerful tool for emotional development, helping children express and regulate their feelings, build self-confidence, and develop resilience in the face of challenges. It allows them to safely explore fears, anxieties, and big emotions, building the capacity to cope with life's ups and downs.

But here's the best part: Play doesn't have to be complicated or expensive. A cardboard box, a set of blocks, a few simple art supplies – these are all you need to unlock a world of learning and growth. A trip to the park, a nature walk, or even a simple pillow fort in the living room can provide endless opportunities for exploration and discovery.

And the most important ingredient? You. Your presence, your participation, and your enthusiasm can transform ordinary playtime into extraordinary learning experiences. Follow your child's lead, get on their level, and join in the fun. Ask open-ended questions like, "What are you building?" or "Tell me about your character," to encourage them to think creatively and express their ideas. Offer gentle suggestions, but avoid taking over or directing the play. Let your child be the leader, and you'll be amazed at what they come up with.

In Action: Playful Learning in Action 

✓ The Budding Architect: Noah, a curious five-year-old, wasn't interested in traditional toys. His room was filled with stuffed animals, but building blocks were his true passion. He'd spend hours meticulously constructing elaborate towers, bridges, and even entire cityscapes. Noah's parents recognized the educational value of his play and encouraged it. They provided him with different building sets, offering challenges appropriate for his age and skill level. They'd join him on the floor, asking open-ended questions like, "What are you building today?" or "How tall can we make this tower before it falls?" These conversations sparked Noah's creativity and encouraged him to articulate his plans and problem-solving strategies. Beyond blocks, Noah's parents transformed everyday household items into playthings. Cardboard boxes became rockets or cars, and blankets morphed into tunnels or forts. Through play, Noah developed strong spatial reasoning skills, mastered concepts like balance and cause-and-effect, and boosted his creativity and imagination.

The Shy Scientist: Maya, a reserved four-year-old, preferred solitary play. She'd often occupy herself with quiet activities like coloring or sorting her collection of pebbles. Maya's parents wanted to nurture her curiosity and encourage interactive play. They introduced open-ended science experiments like mixing baking soda and vinegar to create colorful eruptions or planting seeds and observing their growth. These activities sparked Maya's interest in the world around her. As she experimented, her parents narrated their actions, labeling objects and processes. This laid the foundation for her language development and scientific thinking. Gradually, Maya started including her stuffed animals in her play, pretending to be a veterinarian caring for her patients. This transition from solitary to imaginative play encouraged her to develop a narrative and express herself more verbally. Through play-based learning, Maya overcame her shyness, discovered her fascination with science, and developed important communication and social skills.

Cultivating Emotional Intelligence: Helping Your Child Understand and Express Themselves

Remember those days when your preschooler's biggest worries were whether the blue cup or the red cup held their juice? Now, their emotional landscape is expanding as rapidly as their vocabulary. They're not just happy or sad anymore; they're experiencing a whole kaleidoscope of feelings – from frustration and excitement to jealousy and pride. It's a beautiful, messy, and sometimes overwhelming time for both you and your child.

But here's the good news: You have the power to be their emotional compass, guiding them through this uncharted territory with empathy, understanding, and a whole lot of patience. You can help them develop the essential skills of emotional intelligence (EQ) – the ability to recognize, understand, and manage their own emotions, and recognize and respond to the emotions of others.

Think of it like this: emotions are like weather patterns. Some days are sunny and bright, filled with joy and laughter. Other days are stormy and turbulent, with thunderclouds of anger or sadness rolling in. Just like we teach our children about the weather, we can teach them about emotions – what they are, why we feel them, and how to express them in healthy ways.

This starts with labeling emotions. When your child is upset, instead of saying, "Don't cry," try saying something like:

- **"I see you're feeling frustrated because you can't reach that toy. Would you like me to help you?"** (Identifies frustration and offers solutions)
- **"It looks like you're feeling disappointed that your tower fell. Let's rebuild it together!"** (Identifies disappointment and offers support)
- **"You seem a little shy around the new kids. It's okay to feel nervous sometimes. Maybe we can wave hello together?"** (Identifies shyness and offers comfort/encouragement)

Encourage your child to express their emotions in ways that are safe and appropriate. If they're angry, suggest drawing an angry picture, stomping their feet, or hitting a pillow instead of hitting a sibling. If they're sad, offer a hug, read a comforting story, or let them cry it out. There's no such thing as a "bad" emotion. All feelings are valid, and it's our job to help our children learn how to cope with them in healthy and constructive ways.

But emotional intelligence isn't just about recognizing and expressing our own emotions; it's also about understanding the emotions of others. Talk to your child about how their actions might affect others. For example, if they snatch a toy from a friend, explain that this might make their friend feel sad or angry. Encourage them to put themselves in their friend's shoes and imagine how they would feel. Ask questions like, "How would you feel if someone did that to you?" to spark their empathy.

Books, stories, and even movies can be great tools for exploring emotions. Choose stories with characters who experience a wide range of feelings, and talk to your child about how those characters might be feeling and why. You can also use role-playing activities to help your child practice different ways of responding to emotions. For example, you could pretend to be a friend who is feeling sad and ask your child how they would comfort you. While fostering a love for stories and imaginative play is key, here are some practical strategies you can use to actively build your child's emotional intelligence (EQ):

- **Model Emotional Expression:** Be open about your feelings, labeling them for your child. "I'm feeling frustrated because I can't find my keys."
- **Validate Their Feelings:** Let your child know that it's okay to feel all sorts of emotions, even negative ones. "It's okay to be angry, but we don't hit. Let's find another way to show how you're feeling."
- **Help Them Problem-Solve:** When they're struggling with a difficult emotion, help them brainstorm solutions. "What can we do to help you feel better?"
- **Celebrate Emotional Milestones:** Just as you celebrate physical milestones, acknowledge your child's emotional growth. "You were

really patient waiting for your turn today!"

- **Use "Feeling Faces":** Create or purchase a set of "feeling faces" cards or charts with different facial expressions representing various emotions. Use these as visual aids to help your child identify and label their own feelings and the feelings of others.

Building emotional intelligence is a journey, not a destination. There will be ups and downs, setbacks, and breakthroughs. But by creating a safe space for your child to explore their emotions, you're giving them a gift that will last a lifetime – the ability to navigate the complex world of feelings with confidence, empathy, and resilience.

As your little one's emotional vocabulary expands, so too will their desire to test their limits and explore their growing independence. In the next section, we'll delve into how to cultivate a sense of "I can do it!" by nurturing your preschooler's confidence and encouraging them to take on new challenges with enthusiasm and a can-do spirit.

Make it Happen: Building Emotional Bridges 

✓ Level Up Your Parenthood Even More:

- **Use "I" Statements:** Model healthy communication by using "I" statements to express your own feelings. "I feel frustrated when the toys are scattered everywhere."
- **Read Books About Emotions:** There are many wonderful children's books that address topics like anger, sadness, and jealousy.
- **Create a Safe Space:** Make sure your child feels comfortable expressing their emotions without fear of judgment.

Nurturing Your Preschooler's Confidence:
Fostering a 'Can-Do' Attitude

Picture this: your preschooler is determined to zip up their own jacket, even though their little fingers fumble with the zipper. Instead of swooping in to do it for them (which, let's be honest, is often the quicker route!), you offer encouragement and guidance. "I see you're working hard on that zipper. Start at the bottom and pull it up slowly." After a few tries, with a triumphant grin, they conquer the zipper! That moment of accomplishment, that "I did it!" feeling is pure gold for building confidence.

So, how can you foster this "can-do" attitude in your preschooler? It all starts with letting go of the reins a little. Allow your child to take on age-appropriate tasks and responsibilities, even if it means things might take a little longer or get a little messy. Let them help you with chores like setting the table or sorting laundry. Encourage them to dress themselves, even if their outfit isn't perfectly coordinated, and let them make simple choices, like which book to read at bedtime or what snack to have. These small acts of independence can make a big difference in their self-esteem.

Of course, this doesn't mean leaving them to fend for themselves. Be there to offer guidance and support, but resist the urge to take over. Instead of saying, "Let me do it, you're not doing it right," try saying, "I can see you're trying your best. Do you want me to show you a different way?" This shows your child that you believe in their abilities and encourages them to keep trying, even when things get tough.

Praise effort over outcome. Instead of saying, "You're so smart!" try saying, "Wow, you worked really hard on that drawing! I love all the colors you used." This shifts the focus from innate ability to effort and perseverance, which are essential ingredients for building lasting confidence. Focus on the process, not just the end result.

on't be afraid to let your child fail. Mistakes are simply learning opportunities in disguise. When your child spills their milk, resist the urge to scold or clean it up for them. Instead, hand them a towel and say, "Oops, it looks like we had a spill. Can you help me clean it up?" This teaches them that mistakes happen, but they can be overcome with a little effort and that they are capable of contributing to solutions. Resilience is born from facing and overcoming challenges.

And remember, one of the most powerful ways to build confidence is through unconditional love and acceptance. Let your child know that you love them no matter what, even when they make mistakes or fall short of their goals. This creates a safe space for them to explore, experiment, and take risks without fear of judgment or rejection. It also helps them develop a healthy sense of self-worth that will serve them well throughout their lives.

The Importance of Self-Talk

As your child grows, they will begin to internalize the messages they hear from you and others. Positive self-talk – the inner dialogue we have with ourselves – plays a crucial role in developing a healthy self-image and a strong sense of self-worth. Encourage your child to use positive affirmations like, "I can do it!" or "I'm proud of myself!"

You can also help them reframe negative self-talk. If they say, "I'm not good at this," respond with, "You're still learning, and that's okay. With practice, you'll get better." By teaching them to challenge negative thoughts and replace them with positive ones, you're giving them a powerful tool for building confidence and resilience.

By empowering your preschooler with age-appropriate responsibilities, encouraging problem-solving, and embracing mistakes as opportunities for growth, you're not just building their confidence; you're equipping them with the tools they need to tackle challenges head-on and emerge as resilient, capable individuals. As they step into new experiences with a "can-do" attitude, you'll witness a newfound sense of self-assuredness that will pave the way for their success in school, friendships, and beyond.

As you continue to foster their growing independence, you'll discover that establishing predictable routines and rituals can be a powerful way to provide stability and security amidst the whirlwind of preschool life. In the next section, we'll delve into the importance of routines and rituals, exploring how they can help your child feel safe, grounded, and ready to take on each new day with confidence and enthusiasm.

In Action: Tiny Triumphs

✓ **The Budding Chef:** Maya, a curious five-year-old, loved helping in the kitchen. However, her initial attempts were often met with frustration. She'd knock over ingredients, struggle with measuring cups, and get discouraged by minor setbacks. Recognizing the importance of fostering independence, Maya's parents offered age-appropriate tasks and avoided taking over. They provided her with a safe stepping stool so she could reach the counter and gave her child-safe utensils for stirring and mixing. They focused on praising her effort, saying things like, "Wow, you're measuring so carefully!" or "I love how colorful your salad looks!" Instead of criticizing spills, they presented them as learning opportunities, saying things like, "Oops, looks like we had a spill. Can you help me get a paper towel?" Gradually, with patience and encouragement, Maya's confidence grew in the kitchen. She learned valuable life skills, persevered through challenges, and developed a sense of accomplishment as she mastered new tasks.

✓ **The Hesitant Artist:** Ethan, a shy four-year-old, approached art time with trepidation. Worried his drawings wouldn't be "good enough," he often refused to participate. Ethan's parents wanted to nurture his creativity and build his confidence.

They focused on the joy of exploring art materials, not a perfect end product. They provided him with crayons, paints, and paper, and encouraged him to explore. Instead of dictating what to draw, they used open-ended questions like, "What colors do you see?" or "Show me your favorite animal!" When Ethan expressed dissatisfaction with his work, they offered positive affirmations. They'd say things like, "Wow, you used so many colors!" or "Look how happy your drawing makes you feel!" They also reframed mistakes as learning opportunities, saying things like, "Everyone makes mistakes, that's how we learn new things!" Over time, with encouragement and a focus on fun, Ethan's confidence grew. He began experimenting freely, his fear of failure replaced by a sense of enjoyment. He'd proudly display his creations, a genuine smile on his face. His parents realized they weren't just fostering an artist, but a love of learning and the courage to try new things.

The Importance of Routines and Rituals:
Routines and Rituals for Preschoolers

Gone are the days when your baby's schedule revolved solely around feeding, napping, and diaper changes. As your child blossoms into the preschool years, routines still play a vital role, but they transform into something more meaningful and intentional. Now, routines and rituals become the comforting pillars that hold up your child's day, providing a sense of predictability, security, and belonging.

Imagine your child's world without routines. Mornings would be scrambled attempts to find clothes, rushed breakfasts, and meltdowns over misplaced shoes. A well-established morning routine, perhaps involving picking out clothes the night before, a consistent breakfast ritual, and a clear plan for getting out the door, can make mornings flow smoothly and set the tone for a positive day. Bedtime routines are equally important, serving as a calming bridge between the day's whirlwind of activity and a restful night's sleep. A relaxing bath, the joy of shared stories, and the familiar comfort of a lullaby all contribute to a predictable and positive bedtime experience.

Routines aren't confined to mornings and evenings; they encompass the whole day. Think about mealtimes. Designated times for meals, along with a calm and inviting atmosphere, can make these moments not only nourishing but enjoyable for the whole family.

However, life with a preschooler isn't about rigid schedules. There will be days when the best-laid plans go awry, and that's okay. Be flexible and adaptable, like a willow tree bending in the breeze. The key is to find a balance that works for your unique family and strive for consistency most of the time.

Now, let's weave some magic into your day with rituals! These special moments go beyond the practicalities of daily tasks and create a sense of connection and significance. Perhaps it's a unique handshake you share each morning, a silly song that makes handwashing a delight, or a cherished tradition of family game nights on Fridays. Rituals strengthen the invisible threads that bind your family together, creating a tapestry of shared memories and a sense of belonging that your child will treasure. They also provide a comforting anchor, especially during times of change or uncertainty, like starting preschool or welcoming a new sibling. Familiar traditions can remind your child that even when the world feels a little wobbly, some things remain constant, like the warmth and love of family.

So, embrace the power of routines and rituals! As you embark on this journey of creating a secure and loving foundation for your child, here are some helpful tips:

- **Observe your child's natural rhythms.** What time does their energy dip? When are they most hungry? Use these cues to craft a schedule that complements their natural flow. For example, if your little one is a night owl, a super early bedtime might be met with resistance. Instead, adjust the routine to better suit their sleep-wake tendencies.

- **Start small and celebrate milestones.** Don't try to overhaul your entire day overnight. Begin with manageable changes, like creating a simple morning checklist with pictures or establishing a consistent bedtime routine. This gradual approach makes transitions smoother and less overwhelming for everyone.

- **Be flexible and understanding.** Life throws curveballs, and there will be days when the routine needs to bend. Maybe you overslept, or your child is under the weather. Don't sweat it! Adjust as needed, the goal is to create a supportive framework, not a rigid structure that causes stress.

- **Get your child involved!** Empower your child to participate in creating and maintaining routines and rituals. This promotes a sense of ownership and makes them more likely to cooperate. Ask for their input on what they'd like for bedtime snuggles or allow them to choose a fun song to sing while washing hands. Working together fosters a sense of teamwork and makes routines more enjoyable for everyone.

While routines and rituals provide stability, the preschool years are bound to have their share of bumps along the road. Challenges are a natural part of growing up, and we'll tackle those head-on in the next section. We'll explore common hurdles and offer practical strategies and support to help you navigate them with confidence. You are not alone in this journey. With a little understanding and some helpful tools, you can empower your child to navigate through these challenges and thrive.

In Action: Routines for a Smooth Day 

✓ The Chaotic Mornings: Chaos reigned supreme in the Miller household every morning. Emily, a busy mom juggling work and childcare, struggled to get her preschooler, Alex, out the door on time. Mornings were a whirlwind of frantic searching for lost shoes, meltdowns over mismatched socks, and rushed breakfasts eaten on the go. Recognizing the need for structure, Emily decided to implement a morning routine. She involved Alex in the process, creating a visual chart with pictures of morning tasks like getting dressed, eating breakfast, and brushing teeth. They established a designated spot for Alex's belongings, eliminating last-minute searches. Gradually, with predictability and consistency, the mornings became calmer.

Alex knew what to expect and developed a sense of independence in completing his morning tasks. Emily enjoyed a less stressful start to the day, and they could leave the house feeling prepared and on time.

✓ **The Bedtime Battles:** Bedtime was a nightly battleground in the Johnson household. Five-year-old Lily resisted going to bed, demanding "just one more story" or procrastinating with bathroom breaks. Exhausted parents, John and Lisa, decided to create a calming bedtime routine. They established a consistent bedtime and developed a series of relaxing activities like taking a warm bath, reading cozy stories, and singing lullabies. They introduced a special bedtime lovey that provided comfort and security. Over time, with consistency and positive reinforcement, Lily began to look forward to bedtime as a winding-down ritual. The stressful bedtime battles ceased, replaced by a peaceful end to the day.

Mindful Parenting: Decoding Playtime Routine

✓ **Pause & Reflect:**

- Reflect on your own childhood routines and rituals. How did they affect you?
- Describe your current family routines. Are there areas where you could introduce more structure or predictability?
- How can you involve your child more in creating and maintaining routines?

Navigating Preschool Challenges: Common Concerns and Solutions

Preschool is a time of immense growth and wonder for your child, a vibrant tapestry of newfound friendships, burgeoning independence, and expanding knowledge. But let's be honest – it isn't always sunshine and rainbows. Even the most well-adjusted preschooler will face their fair share of challenges, from navigating social dynamics to dealing with big feelings. As parents, you're not just spectators in this adventure; you're the coaches, the cheerleaders, and the occasional referees, ready to guide your child through the ups and downs of this exciting phase.

Picture this: Your once adventurous eater suddenly pushes away anything remotely green on their plate. Or maybe your normally outgoing child seems withdrawn and hesitant to join in playtime. Perhaps even bedtime becomes a battleground, filled with tears and tales of monsters under the bed. These are just a few of the many challenges that can pop up during the preschool years.

But here's the good news: These challenges are normal! They're a sign that your child is growing, learning, and navigating the exciting (and sometimes tricky) world around them. And guess what? You, as their superhero parent/caregiver, are perfectly equipped to help them through it all.

The Picky Eater Adventures: The Great Escape of the Green Beans

Gone are the days when your little explorer gobbled up everything on their plate! Now, they might be giving the green beans a side-eye, or turning their nose up at broccoli. This newfound pickiness can be puzzling, but it's super common for preschoolers. Their taste buds are on a big adventure, discovering new flavors and textures, and sometimes that means familiar favorites get left behind.

The good news is, mealtimes can still be a fun (and healthy!) quest! Try offering a variety of colorful treasures on their plate, like sliced veggies in fun shapes or juicy fruits. You can even turn meal prep into a game! Let your little one help wash the fruits and veggies, or give them a spoon to stir the batter for healthy muffins. Don't get discouraged by initial rejections; it can take multiple exposures for a child to accept a new food. A few chicken nuggets here and there won't hurt. It's about balance and progress, not perfection.

The Big World Outside: Helping Your Preschooler Say Goodbye

The world is getting bigger for your preschooler! This can be exciting, but also a little scary. Sometimes that fear shows up as separation anxiety, that familiar clinginess when it's time to say goodbye. This is a normal part of development, often peaking around 18 months but sometimes lingering into the preschool years.

While seeing your little one upset is tough, remember this is a sign of a healthy attachment. They feel safe and loved with you, and are starting to navigate their growing independence. To ease the transition, create a special goodbye routine, like a high five or a secret handshake. A favorite stuffed animal or blanket can also offer comfort when you're apart. Most importantly, reassure them with lots of love and hugs, and remind them that you'll always come back. If the anxiety persists, talk to your child's teacher or caregiver. They may have additional strategies to help your child feel more comfortable in your absence.

Building Bridges of Friendship

The preschool years are a prime time for developing social skills and forming friendships. However, disagreements, struggles with sharing, and difficulty making new friends are all common challenges that can arise. These social hiccups, while frustrating, are valuable learning opportunities for your child.

Help them develop their social skills by modeling empathy, teaching them how to express their feelings, and encouraging them to take turns and share. Arrange playdates to give them the opportunity to practice these skills in a comfortable setting. If they're having trouble making friends, consider setting up playdates with classmates or enrolling them in activities where they can interact with other children their age. Friendships take time to develop, and it's okay if your child doesn't instantly click with everyone they meet.

Sweet Dreams and Nighttime Fears

Nighttime awakenings and bad dreams can be common in preschoolers. Their vivid imaginations can sometimes lead to scary thoughts and images that make it difficult to fall asleep or stay asleep.

Establishing a consistent bedtime routine, creating a calming sleep environment, and addressing any underlying fears or anxieties can go a long way in promoting restful sleep. Comfort your child if they wake up from a nightmare, reassure them that they're safe, and help them get back to sleep. Consider using a nightlight, reading calming bedtime stories, or even creating a "monster spray" (a simple mixture of water and lavender oil) to help your child feel more secure at night.

Aggression and Biting: Navigating Tricky Terrain

Aggression and biting can be challenging behaviors to manage, but they're not uncommon in preschoolers. These behaviors often stem from frustration, lack of impulse control, or difficulty expressing needs. Your child isn't trying to be "bad," they're simply struggling to manage their emotions and navigate social situations.

To address aggressive behaviors, teach your child alternative ways to express their feelings, such as using words to communicate frustration or taking a break to calm down. Model peaceful conflict resolution and provide positive reinforcement for good behavior. When your child uses their words instead of resorting to physical aggression, make sure to acknowledge and praise their effort.

If biting occurs, calmly separate the children involved and offer comfort to the child who was hurt. Talk to your child about why biting is not okay and explain how it hurts others. Help them find alternative ways to express their emotions, like asking for help or using words to communicate their needs. Consistency and patience are key when addressing these challenging behaviors.

Beyond the Basics: Other Preschool Challenges

Preschoolers might also face other challenges, such as difficulty adjusting to a new routine, potty training setbacks, or anxieties related to starting school. Every child is unique, and their challenges will vary. The key is to be patient, understanding, and supportive.

As your little preschooler prepares to take that exciting leap into elementary school, a new chapter unfolds, filled with exciting milestones and new challenges to conquer. In the next part, we'll shift our focus to the elementary school years, exploring how you can support your child's continued development as they navigate the world of academics, friendships, and personal growth.

In Action: Navigating Preschool Challenges 

✓ The Shy Sprout: Lily, a five-year-old with sparkling eyes and a mop of red curls, loved the comfort of her home routine. However, playdates at the park turned into tearful clinging to her mother's leg, and classroom circle time became an ordeal of whispered answers and downcast eyes. Lily struggled with shyness, preferring the company of her stuffed animals and imaginary friends to the unpredictability of social interaction. Her parents, David and Sarah, worried about her limited social interaction and wanted to help her blossom in group settings. They decided to gently encourage her to step outside her comfort zone. David enrolled Lily in a weekend art class, a small setting focused on exploration and creativity. At first, Lily observed from the sidelines, but the vibrant colors and engaging activities slowly drew her in. The art teacher, Ms.

Chen, was patient and encouraging, providing opportunities for collaboration without pressure. Over time, Lily began to interact with other children, sharing her artwork and giggling over spilled paint. The art class became a safe space for Lily to experiment with social interaction, building confidence and laying the foundation for future friendships.

✓ The Goodbye Grump: Leo, a typically outgoing preschooler, turned into a ball of tears every morning at drop-off. He'd cling to his mother's waist, pleading to stay home. Emily, his mother, felt her heart clench with each goodbye. She tried various tactics, but nothing worked. Desperate for a solution, Emily talked to Leo's teacher, Ms. Rodriguez. Ms. Rodriguez suggested a special goodbye ritual. They created a high-five goodbye routine, where Leo would say, "See you later love you!" This simple act did the trick. The high five became a way for Leo to acknowledge the separation while knowing his mom would return. After a few weeks, the tearful goodbyes vanished, replaced by a confident high five and a skip into the classroom.

Make it Happen: Help Your Child Thrive 

✓ Level Up Your Parenthood:
- Create a Visual Schedule: Develop a picture chart outlining your child's daily routine to ease transitions and manage expectations.
- Involve Your Child: Empower your child to participate in creating routines and choosing calming bedtime rituals.

- **Practice Social Skills at Home:** Role-play scenarios where your child might experience social anxiety, like sharing toys or asking a classmate to play.
- **Offer Choices:** Give your child age-appropriate choices throughout the day to foster a sense of independence and control.
- **Model Empathy and Kindness:** Show your child how to be empathetic and kind to others through your own words and actions.

Part 5:

Fostering Growth:
Elementary School

Inside This Part

As the first day of school approaches, you might feel a mix of emotions. Excitement for the new adventures your child will embark on, a touch of nostalgia as they trade finger painting for fractions, and perhaps a little apprehension about the challenges that lie ahead. This new chapter, however, is as much a growth opportunity for you as it is for your child. Welcome to the elementary school years, a time of incredible transformation and discovery.

In this part, we'll delve into the exciting (and sometimes daunting) world of elementary school, equipping you with the tools and insights you need to support your child's journey. We'll explore the cognitive leaps and bounds they'll make, from mastering reading and writing to developing critical thinking skills. We'll discuss how to foster a love of learning that goes beyond the classroom, creating a home environment where curiosity thrives and exploration is encouraged.

But it's not just academics. We'll also dive into the importance of building strong social skills, nurturing friendships, and developing a resilient mindset that embraces challenges and setbacks. We'll tackle the common hurdles that elementary school children face – from bullies and peer pressure to academic struggles and anxiety – and offer practical strategies for helping your child navigate these complex social and emotional landscapes. You're not just raising a student; you're raising a whole person, and these elementary years are a crucial time for fostering their growth in all aspects of life.

Brain Builders:
Understanding Your Child's Development in Elementary School

The first day of elementary school is a whirlwind of emotions — excitement, nerves, and maybe a touch of nostalgia for nap time. But beneath the surface, something incredible is happening: your child's brain is undergoing a remarkable transformation.

Imagine their brain as a bustling construction site, rapidly building new neural pathways. This period of cognitive growth is phenomenal. Your child will develop the ability to think abstractly, reason logically, and analyze information with greater complexity. They'll move from learning to read to reading to learn, unlocking a world of knowledge and imagination. They'll grapple with concepts like cause and effect, time, and morality, forming the foundation for critical thinking and ethical decision-making. As they explore different subjects and activities, they'll discover their passions, talents, and areas where they might need a little extra help.

Elementary school isn't just about academics. It's a time for emotional and social development. Your child will learn to navigate complex friendships, cope with peer pressure, and develop a sense of self-identity. They'll grasp the consequences of their actions, the importance of responsibility, and the value of perseverance. These skills are crucial for their overall well-being and happiness, alongside academic achievement.

As your child ventures into this new world, your role shifts from primary caregiver to supportive guide. You're no longer the sole source of knowledge and entertainment; you're a partner in their learning journey. Foster curiosity and exploration by creating a home environment that celebrates effort and learning. Simple things like discussing their day, providing engaging materials, and creating opportunities for hands-on learning can make a big difference.

While academics are important, they're just one piece of the puzzle. We'll delve into the emotional and social challenges elementary school children face, such as anxiety, bullying, and peer pressure. We'll offer practical strategies to support them — teaching relaxation techniques for anxiety, role-playing scenarios to deal with bullies, and fostering open communication to discuss peer pressure.

One key concept we'll emphasize is cultivating a growth mindset in your child. This means believing that abilities and intelligence can be developed through effort, learning, and perseverance. (The opposite is a fixed mindset, where abilities are seen as unchangeable.) Research shows that children with a growth mindset are more likely to embrace challenges, persevere through setbacks, and ultimately achieve greater success. By praising your child's effort and progress, emphasizing learning from mistakes, and encouraging them to try new things, you can help them develop this empowering mindset.

Working with your child's teachers and school is crucial for creating a collaborative learning environment. This includes attending parent-teacher conferences, staying informed about their progress, and advocating for their needs. By building a strong partnership with educators, you can ensure that your child receives the support they need to thrive. By understanding your child's development and providing the right support, you can help them build a strong foundation for lifelong learning, social success, and emotional well-being.

Understanding your child's evolving brain equips you with valuable knowledge about their behavior, learning style, and overall development. During the elementary school years, this knowledge empowers you to provide the right kind of support at the right time, creating a nurturing environment where they can flourish. And remember, school isn't just about academics; it's about fostering a lifelong love of learning that extends far beyond the classroom walls.

In the next section, we'll shift our focus to creating a supportive and engaging home environment that sparks your child's curiosity, fuels their imagination, and nurtures a love of learning that will grow and evolve alongside them.

In Action: Navigating Elementary School Challenges 

✓ **The Friendship Flurry:** Ethan, a bright and energetic eight-year-old, thrived in academia. However, the social playground proved to be a trickier terrain. He struggled to navigate the complexities of friendships, often left on the sidelines during lunchtime games. Ethan's parents, Michael and Lisa, noticed his dejection and decided to gently explore the situation. Through open communication, they learned that Ethan often jumped into games without being invited, leading to frustration from his peers. Michael and Lisa helped Ethan develop social cues, teaching him the importance of asking to join a game and respecting others' boundaries. They also enrolled him in an improv comedy class, where Ethan blossomed in a supportive environment focused on collaboration and communication. The improv class provided opportunities to practice social skills in a fun and low-pressure setting. Ethan gradually gained confidence in reading social cues and initiating interactions appropriately. Soon, lunchtimes became filled with laughter and the joy of friendship.

The Budding Mathematician: Sarah, a quiet and curious nine-year-old, loved spending hours lost in the world of books. While her creativity flourished in language arts class, math presented a daunting challenge. Sarah would shut down during math lessons, frustrated by the abstract concepts. Her teacher, Ms. Jackson, recognized Sarah's potential and her learning style. Ms. Jackson incorporated manipulatives like blocks and counters into her lessons, transforming abstract problems into tangible experiences that Sarah could connect with. She also encouraged Sarah to explain her thought process, helping her identify areas where she got stuck. At home, Sarah's parents, David and Anne, embraced a growth mindset. They praised Sarah's effort and persistence, emphasizing that math skills could be developed through practice and learning from mistakes. Together, they explored online math games and real-world applications of math concepts, like baking cookies and calculating ingredients. With patient guidance, a supportive learning environment, and a growth mindset, Sarah's confidence in math began to blossom.

Fostering a Love of Learning:
Creating a Supportive Learning Environment

Imagine stepping into your child's world, where every day holds the promise of new discoveries. The rustling leaves outside become a science lesson, the grocery list a chance to practice letters, and a simple cardboard box a portal to a magical kingdom. As your child enters elementary school, your home becomes the foundation upon which their love of learning is built. It's a space where curiosity is cultivated, creativity flourishes, and the joy of discovery takes center stage.

But what does it truly mean to "foster a love of learning?" It's not about drilling facts or pushing for perfect grades. It's about nurturing an insatiable curiosity, a thirst for knowledge, and a genuine enjoyment of the learning process. It's about creating an environment where your child feels safe to explore, experiment, and even make mistakes. By instilling this love of learning, you're not just setting them up for academic success; you're giving them the tools to become lifelong learners who are adaptable, resourceful, and passionate about the world around them.

Think of yourselves as co-explorers on this exciting adventure. Ask open-ended questions that spark curiosity: "Why do you think the sky is blue?" "How does a plant grow?" "What do you want to learn about today?" Engage in conversations about your child's interests, passions, and even their frustrations. Listen attentively to their ideas, validate their feelings, and encourage them to ask questions and seek answers. Be genuinely interested in what they have to say, even if it's about the latest video game or cartoon character. Even seemingly trivial topics can open doors to deeper conversations and learning opportunities.

Your home is more than just a place to live; it's a learning laboratory. Stock your shelves with books on a variety of topics, not just those assigned for school. Offer art supplies, building materials, and science kits for creative expression and hands-on exploration. Make space for messy experiments and encourage your child to build, create, and invent.

Transform everyday activities into learning opportunities. Cook together, incorporating math skills as you measure ingredients and science concepts as you explain how baking soda makes a cake rise. Read maps and plan family trips, sparking conversations about geography and history. Play board games that encourage strategic thinking and problem-solving. Visit museums and libraries, allowing your child to discover new interests and explore different worlds.

Don't underestimate the power of your enthusiasm. When you show genuine excitement about learning new things, your child will naturally follow suit. Read aloud to them, even as they get older and become independent readers themselves share interesting facts you've learned, and celebrate their discoveries, no matter how small. Let them see that learning is a lifelong adventure, filled with joy, wonder, and endless possibilities. By modeling a love of learning, you'll inspire your child to become a lifelong learner.

As your child navigates the academic world, remember that learning isn't just about grades and test scores. It's about fostering a deep connection to knowledge, a thirst for understanding, and a sense of joy in discovery. Here's how additionally you can support this journey by:

- **Creating a Routine:** Establish a consistent study time and homework routine. This helps your child develop good study habits, manage their time effectively, and reduce stress around schoolwork. Consider creating a designated study space, free from distractions, where they can focus on their learning.
- **Being a Learning Partner:** Offer help with homework when needed, but don't simply give them the answers. Ask guiding questions that encourage them to think through the problem and discover solutions on their own. This helps them develop problem-solving skills and critical thinking.
- **Connecting Learning to Life:** Help your child see the relevance of what they're learning in school to the real world. If they're studying ancient Egypt, visit a museum exhibit or watch a documentary together. Discuss current events and help them understand how academic concepts apply to real-life situations.

- **Celebrating Mistakes:** When your child makes a mistake, view it as a learning opportunity rather than a failure. Help them analyze what went wrong and brainstorm solutions. This promotes a growth mindset and teaches them that setbacks are a natural part of the learning process.
- **Encouraging Curiosity:** Take your child's questions seriously and help them find answers. Visit the library, research online together, or conduct simple experiments to satisfy their curiosity. A curious mind is a powerful mind!

By creating a supportive learning environment at home, you're not just helping your child succeed in school; you're nurturing a lifelong love of learning that will enrich their lives in countless ways.

As your child's love of learning blossoms, you'll also notice their thinking skills sharpen. They'll start to ask "why" more often, question assumptions, and seek out answers to their burning curiosities. This natural progression sets the stage for developing critical thinking and problem-solving skills, which are essential for navigating the complexities of life. In the next section, we'll delve into these vital skills, exploring how you can empower your child to become an independent thinker, a creative problem-solver, and a lifelong learner. Get ready to witness their minds expand and their capabilities soar!

In Action: Cultivating a Love of Learning 

- The Hesitant Historian: Liam, a bookish and introverted ten-year-old, found solace in the fictional worlds he devoured through his beloved novels. However, history class felt like a foreign land to him, filled with dates, names, and seemingly endless memorization. Liam's disengagement worried his parents and teacher, Ms. Brown. Determined to ignite Liam's interest in history, Ms. Brown incorporated more interactive learning strategies. Field trips to historical landmarks brought the past to life, and classroom debates encouraged critical thinking about historical events. Liam found himself captivated by the lively discussions. Ms. Brown also introduced historical fiction novels, allowing Liam to connect with the past through a familiar and engaging format. Gradually, Liam's perspective on history shifted. He began to see it not as a collection of facts but as a story filled with adventure, drama, and the complexities of human behavior. Liam's love of reading morphed into a fascination with the real stories behind the fictional accounts.

Make it Happen: Learning Adventures 

✓ **Level Up Your Parenthood:**
  - **Embrace Playful Learning:** Integrate learning into everyday activities. Bake cookies together to practice fractions, or measure ingredients for a science experiment.
  - **Limit Screen Time:** Set clear boundaries on screen time to promote active play, creative pursuits, and hands-on learning experiences.
  - **Connect Learning to Life:** Help your child see the relevance of what they're learning in school to the real world. Discuss current events and explore how academic concepts apply to real-life situations.

- **Visit Museums and Libraries:** Make regular trips to museums and libraries, allowing your child to discover new interests and explore different worlds.
- **Read Aloud Together:** Don't stop reading aloud to your child just because they can read independently. Choose age-appropriate books that spark conversation and ignite a love of literature.
- **Become a Learning Partner:** Offer help with homework when needed, but don't simply give them the answers. Ask guiding questions that encourage them to think through the problem and discover solutions on their own.
- **Embrace Nature:** Spend time outdoors exploring nature. Go for walks in the park, hike in the woods, or plant a garden.
- **Incorporate Games and Activities:** Board games, puzzles, and even charades can be fantastic ways to reinforce critical thinking, problem-solving, and social skills in a fun and engaging way.

Developing Critical Thinking and Problem-Solving Skills:
Fostering Independent Thinkers and Effective Problem Solvers

Remember those endless "why" questions your curious toddler peppered you with? Well, get ready for round two – the elementary school edition! As your child's brain continues to develop, their capacity for critical thinking and problem-solving will soar. They'll begin to question assumptions, analyze information, and seek out innovative solutions to challenges, all while forging their own unique path of understanding.

Imagine your child as a detective, piecing together clues, examining evidence, and drawing conclusions. They might be trying to figure out how a toy works, design a winning strategy for a board game, or navigate a conflict with a friend. These seemingly simple tasks are actually complex cognitive processes that require critical thinking and problem-solving skills.

As parents, we can actively nurture these skills by encouraging our children to think for themselves. Instead of always providing the answers, pose thought-provoking questions that spark their curiosity and challenge them to think critically. "Why do you think that happened?" "What are some different ways we could solve this problem?" "What would happen if we tried this instead?" Let them grapple with questions and explore various avenues of thought, even if their initial ideas seem outlandish. There's no single "right" answer when it comes to problem-solving.

Encourage them to see things from different perspectives and consider alternative solutions. Ask them to explain their reasoning and help them weigh the pros and cons of different choices. This helps them develop the ability to think flexibly, evaluate information, and make informed decisions. Encourage them to consider the impact of their choices on themselves and others, fostering a sense of responsibility and accountability.

Creating opportunities for hands-on learning is also key. Whether it's building a model airplane, designing a science experiment, or coding a simple computer program, these activities encourage children to apply their knowledge, think creatively, and find solutions to real-world problems. Let them tinker, explore, and get their hands dirty! These experiences not only build critical thinking skills but also ignite a passion for learning and discovery.

Don't underestimate the power of play! Board games, puzzles, and even imaginative play scenarios can all help children develop critical thinking and problem-solving skills. Encourage them to brainstorm ideas, collaborate with others, and persevere through challenges. Through play, children learn to negotiate, compromise, and think strategically – skills that are invaluable in both personal and professional life.

It's also important to model these skills yourself. Let your child see you working through problems, considering different options, and making decisions based on careful analysis. Talk to them about your thought process, and invite them to share their own ideas and perspectives. When you make a mistake, show them how you learn from it and adapt your approach. Demonstrate that it's okay to not have all the answers and that the process of figuring things out is just as important as the final outcome.

Fostering critical thinking and problem-solving skills is not about teaching your child to always get the "right" answer. It's about nurturing their curiosity, encouraging them to ask questions, and empowering them to find their own solutions. It's about cultivating a growth mindset that embraces challenges and sees mistakes as opportunities for learning.

Critical thinking and problem-solving are not just logic and reason. Creativity also plays a crucial role. Encourage your child to think outside the box, brainstorm unconventional ideas, and embrace their unique perspective. Creative thinking often leads to innovative solutions and a deeper understanding of the world around them. Provide them with opportunities for creative expression, such as art projects, music, or writing. Celebrate their unique ideas and encourage them to take risks and explore new possibilities.

Help your child see the relevance of critical thinking and problem-solving skills in their everyday lives. Encourage them to apply these skills to real-world situations, such as planning a family outing, deciding how to spend their allowance, or resolving a conflict with a sibling. By connecting these skills to practical experiences, you'll help them understand their value and develop the confidence to use them in a variety of contexts.

Inevitably, your child will encounter challenges and setbacks along the way. That's okay! It's how they respond to these challenges that matter. Help them develop resilience by encouraging them to persevere, learn from their mistakes, and try again. Remind them of past successes and help them break down complex problems into smaller, more manageable steps.

By providing a supportive and stimulating environment, you can help your child develop the cognitive tools they need to thrive in school, the workplace, and in life. As they become more independent thinkers and problem-solvers, they'll also be developing the social skills necessary to collaborate, respect others, and build strong relationships. In the next section, we'll delve deeper into how to foster these crucial social skills, ensuring that your child is not only a bright mind, but also a kind and compassionate heart.

In Action: Cultivating Critical Thinkers 

✓ The Hesitant Scientist: Anna, a cautious and detail-oriented nine-year-old, preferred following instructions to the letter in science class. While she excelled at replicating experiments with precision, she struggled with open-ended projects that required independent thinking and creative problem-solving. During a science fair project on water filtration, Anna meticulously followed the teacher's instructions, hesitant to deviate from the established method.

Her science teacher, Mr. Wang, recognized Anna's potential and gently nudged her to explore different approaches. Mr. Wang encouraged Anna to research alternative filtration materials and experiment with different construction methods. He emphasized that mistakes were opportunities to learn and refine her ideas.

With Mr. Wang's guidance, Anna gained confidence in experimenting and troubleshooting. Her final project showcased a unique and effective water filtration system, a result of her careful observation, critical thinking, and newfound willingness to embrace creative solutions.

Mindful Parenting: Cultivate Critical Thinkers

✓ **Pause & Reflect:**

- Think about a subject you struggled with in school. How could a more engaging learning environment have changed your experience?
- How can you encourage your child to think outside the box and embrace creative solutions?
- How can you better connect your child's interests to their learning experiences?

Building Social Skills and Friendships: Fostering Collaboration, Respect, and Responsibility

Remember those early playdates filled with parallel play – your child happily building their own block tower while another child focused on a puzzle, both seemingly oblivious to the other's presence? As children enter elementary school, their social world expands, and with it, their desire for interaction and connection deepens. It's a fascinating journey to witness as they discover the joy of sharing, cooperating, and building lasting friendships.

Think of social skills as a secret language that allows your child to connect with others, express their needs, and navigate the complexities of human relationships. It's like a toolbox filled with essential tools – empathy, communication, compromise, and respect – that they'll use throughout their lives.

You might notice your child's social interactions evolving. They might start initiating playdates, sharing toys more readily, or showing concern for a friend's feelings. They might also encounter new challenges, like disagreements, hurt feelings, and exclusion. These experiences, while sometimes difficult, are invaluable opportunities for growth and learning.

As parents, you play a crucial role in guiding your child through this social maze. You can model healthy social interactions, teach them how to express their feelings in words and help them navigate conflicts with empathy and understanding. By fostering a sense of collaboration, respect, and responsibility, you're not just preparing them for the playground; you're equipping them with the skills they need to thrive in relationships, school, and the workplace.

Imagine a typical elementary school scenario: your child and their friend are both vying for the same role in a game. Instead of jumping to resolve the conflict, step back and observe. Can they work it out on their own? If not, gently guide them towards a solution. "It looks like you both want to be the leader. How about you take turns? You can be the leader for the first round, and then your friend can be the leader for the next round." If they can't agree on a solution, offer a third option: "Maybe you can come up with a new game where you both get to be leaders."

Help your child understand the importance of taking turns, sharing, and respecting other people's feelings. Encourage them to use "I" statements to express their needs and desires, rather than blaming or accusing others. For instance, instead of saying, "You're being mean!" they could say, "I feel sad when you don't include me in the game." This helps them take ownership of their emotions and communicate in a way that's more likely to be heard.

Social skills are not just about playing nicely with others; they're also about taking responsibility for one's actions and contributing to the community.

Encourage your child to help with chores around the house, participate in group projects at school, and volunteer in their community. These experiences teach them the value of teamwork, collaboration, and making a positive impact on the world. By contributing to something bigger than themselves, they learn that their actions matter and that they can make a difference.

In the elementary years, friendships deepen and become more complex. Your child might start forming close bonds with a few special friends, experiencing the joy of shared secrets, inside jokes, and unwavering loyalty. They might also encounter the sting of rejection, betrayal, or hurt feelings. As a parent, you can support your child's friendships by creating opportunities for social interaction, encouraging them to invite friends over, and facilitating playdates and group activities. Talk to them about the qualities of a good friend, like loyalty, honesty, and kindness. Help them understand that healthy friendships involve give-and-take and that conflicts are a normal part of any relationship.

If your child is shy or introverted, remember that it's simply their personality, not a flaw. Help them build social confidence by creating opportunities for interaction in small, low-pressure settings. Encourage them to join clubs or activities that align with their interests, where they can connect with others who share their passions. Celebrate their small victories, such as initiating a conversation or joining a group activity, and remind them that they are valued and loved for who they are.

Elementary school friendships can be difficult to navigate, with their fair share of ups and downs. Teach your child how to cope with rejection, resolve conflicts peacefully, and stand up for themselves when necessary. Help them understand that not every friendship will last forever and that it's okay to outgrow certain relationships.

By equipping your child with these essential social tools, you're not just preparing them for the playground or the classroom; you're giving them a strong foundation for building meaningful connections, healthy relationships, and personal fulfillment throughout their lives.

But remember, strong social skills are only part of the puzzle. A child's sense of self-worth and confidence play an equally vital role in their overall development. In the next section, we'll explore how you can empower your child to develop a positive self-image, a belief in their abilities, and the resilience to overcome challenges with grace and determination.

Make it Happen: Confidence Through Connection 

✓ Level Up Your Parenthood:
- **Encourage Social Interaction:** Create opportunities for your child to interact with other children, such as playdates, group activities, or team sports.
- **Model Healthy Social Interactions:** Show your child how to greet others, take turns, share toys, and resolve conflicts peacefully.
- **Teach Empathy and Emotional Language:** Help your child understand and identify emotions in themselves and others. Encourage them to use "I" statements to express

their feelings.

- Celebrate Cooperation and Teamwork: Highlight the benefits of working together and achieving common goals.
- Praise Effort and Perseverance: Encourage your child to try new things, even if they feel shy or nervous at first. Celebrate their efforts and progress in building social skills.

Developing Self-Esteem and Confidence:
Building a Strong Self-Image

Remember those chubby finger paintings proudly displayed on the refrigerator? Those early artistic endeavors were more than just colorful messes – they were a testament to your child's burgeoning creativity and confidence. Fast forward to elementary school, and that same confidence is taking on a new form. The world has gotten bigger, filled with complex subjects, social interactions, and a growing sense of self. As parents, our role becomes one of guiding and supporting them as they navigate this exciting, and sometimes challenging, new landscape.

Imagine your child's self-esteem as a beautiful garden. We, as parents, are the gardeners, nurturing the seeds of confidence and self-worth. Here are some ways we can cultivate that garden together:

- **Celebrate the little victories.** Acing a spelling test, mastering a new skill on the playground, or simply finishing a challenging homework assignment – these are all moments worth celebrating. Our enthusiastic praise lets them know we see their effort and hard work, and that builds confidence. Be specific in your praise! Instead of a generic "good job," point out the specific steps they took or the challenges they overcame. For example, "I loved how you sounded out those new words in the spelling test!" or "You practiced that jump shot all week, and it really paid off today!"

- **Focus on progress, not perfection.** Elementary school is a time of learning and exploration. There will be mistakes, and that's okay! Use setbacks as teachable moments. Talk through what went wrong, and help them develop strategies to improve next time. The message you want to send is that effort and perseverance matter more than getting everything right the first time. Help them reframe mistakes as learning opportunities. You can say, "Everyone makes mistakes! What can we learn from this so you can do even better next time?"

- **Expose them to new challenges.** Encourage them to try new activities, whether it's joining a sports team, taking an art class, or learning a musical instrument. Stepping outside their comfort zone can be scary, but it's also a great way to build confidence and discover hidden talents. Be their biggest cheerleader – offer encouragement and support along the way, but let them take ownership of their experience. Help them identify their interests and find activities that align with them. This increases the chances they'll stick with it and experience the satisfaction of achievement.

- **Help them find their tribe.** Strong friendships provide a sense of belonging and acceptance, which is crucial for developing self-esteem. Encourage them to connect with classmates who share their interests, and help them navigate social situations. Role-playing scenarios or discussing social cues can equip them with the tools they need to build positive relationships. Model positive social interactions yourself. Show your child how to greet others, take turns in conversation, and be a good listener.

- **Embrace their individuality.** Every child is unique, with their own strengths, weaknesses, and interests. Our job is to celebrate those differences, not try to mold them into someone they're not. When we accept and appreciate them for who they are, it empowers them to do the same. Help them identify their strengths and find ways to showcase them. This could be through participating in a school play, joining a debate team, or volunteering for a cause they care about.

- **Build a growth mindset together.** A growth mindset is the belief that intelligence and abilities can be developed through effort, learning, and perseverance. Talk to your child about the brain being like a muscle that grows stronger the more you use it. Celebrate their effort and persistence, not just their achievements (more on growth mindset in the next section).

Building self-esteem is a journey, not a destination. There will be ups and downs along the way. They'll face challenges, make mistakes, and experience setbacks. It's during these moments that resilience becomes key. The important thing is to be there for them, offering encouragement, celebrating their victories, and helping them learn from their mistakes. With our love and support, they'll blossom into confident, capable individuals who are ready to embrace the world.

In the next section, we'll explore the concept of a growth mindset, a powerful tool that can help your child bounce back from setbacks, embrace challenges, and learn from their mistakes. We'll share practical tips and strategies to foster this growth mindset in your child, setting them up for success not just in elementary school, but throughout their lives.

In Action: Cultivating Confidence

The Budding Ballerina: Sarah, a bright and energetic seven-year-old, dreamt of twirling across the stage in a tutu. Enthralled by the grace and poise of the ballerinas she saw in books and movies, she yearned to join a dance class. However, self-doubt held her back. "What if I'm not good enough?" she worried, her confidence waning at the thought of unfamiliar steps and potential missteps. Her parents, recognizing Sarah's internal struggle, encouraged her to embrace the challenge. They talked about the growth mindset, explaining that everyone starts somewhere and that practice and perseverance lead to improvement. They signed her up for a beginner's ballet class, emphasizing the joy of learning and self-expression rather than achieving perfection. Initially nervous, Sarah found comfort in the supportive atmosphere of the class. With each week, her confidence grew alongside her skills. The supportive environment and emphasis on progress over perfection allowed Sarah to blossom, her initial anxieties replaced by a newfound sense of accomplishment and pride.

✓ The Reluctant Reader: David, a ten-year-old with a vivid imagination, loved building elaborate Lego creations over getting lost in books. Decoding unfamiliar words felt like a chore, hindering his enjoyment of reading. This negative self-image affected his motivation to even try. Aware of his challenges, David's parents implemented strategies to foster a love of reading. They chose books aligned with his interests – graphic novels or stories about robots and inventions. Audiobooks became part of bedtime, allowing David to experience stories without the struggle of words. Gradually, narratives drew him in, and his imagination was sparked by characters and plots. With patient encouragement and newfound confidence, David tackled chapter books, his fluency and comprehension improving steadily.

Building Resilience:
Embracing Challenges and Learning from Mistakes (Growth Mindset)

Picture your child beaming with pride after scoring a goal in soccer, or eagerly showing you a "100%" on their spelling test. These moments of triumph are wonderful, aren't they? But what happens when things don't go as planned? When the goal is missed or the test results aren't stellar? How your child reacts to these setbacks reveals their resilience—their ability to bounce back from challenges and keep moving forward.

Resilience isn't about avoiding setbacks altogether; it's about learning how to navigate them. It's the ability to dust yourself off after a fall, to try again when things get tough, and to see failures not as roadblocks, but as stepping stones on the path to success. Think of resilience as the emotional and mental armor that protects your child from life's inevitable bumps and bruises. It's the ability to adapt, persevere, and emerge stronger from adversity. Resilience is the compass that guides them through life's storms, helping them find their way back to calmer waters.

The key to building resilience lies in fostering a growth mindset—the belief that abilities and intelligence can be developed through dedication and hard work. When children believe that they can improve, they're more likely to embrace challenges, persevere in the face of setbacks, and ultimately achieve their goals. This mindset is a powerful antidote to the fear of failure, turning mistakes into opportunities for learning and growth.

As parents, you can cultivate a growth mindset in your child by focusing on effort and progress rather than just outcomes. Instead of praising their intelligence ("You're so smart!"), praise their hard work and determination ("I'm so proud of how hard you studied for that test"). When they make mistakes, help them see those mistakes as opportunities for learning and growth, rather than as failures. "Mistakes are proof that you are trying," is a powerful message to convey to your child. Help them understand that even the most successful people have made countless mistakes along the way, and those mistakes were essential stepping stones to their achievements.

Encourage your child to take on challenges, even if they don't succeed at first. Remind them that everyone makes mistakes, and that's how we learn and grow. Teach them to embrace challenges as opportunities to learn new skills and develop their abilities. "What can we learn from this experience?" is a question that can open up a world of possibility and growth.

Provide them with age-appropriate challenges that push their limits but are still achievable. Whether it's learning a new skill, tackling a complex puzzle, or participating in a competition, these experiences can help them build confidence, perseverance, and a sense of accomplishment.

It's also important to model resilience yourself. Let your child see you facing challenges head-on, making mistakes, and learning from them. Share your own experiences of overcoming obstacles and how they made you stronger. When your child sees that you're not afraid of failure, they'll be more likely to embrace challenges themselves. Share stories of your own setbacks and how you persevered, emphasizing the importance of not giving up. Talk about the strategies you used to cope with difficult situations and how you ultimately learned from your experiences.

Another key aspect of resilience is self-compassion. Teach your child to be kind to themselves when things don't go as planned. Help them understand that everyone has strengths and weaknesses and that it's okay to not be good at everything. Encourage them to focus on their strengths and celebrate their accomplishments, no matter how small. Let them know that you love them unconditionally and that your love is not based on their achievements. Help them develop a positive self-talk habit, replacing negative thoughts with affirmations like, "I can do hard things," or "I'm proud of myself for trying."

Building resilience also involves creating a supportive and encouraging environment at home. Offer your child opportunities to take risks, try new things, and step outside their comfort zones. Allow them to make choices and decisions, and help them problem-solve when they encounter obstacles. When they experience setbacks, offer empathy and support, but also encourage them to find their own solutions. This fosters a sense of agency and empowers them to take ownership of their challenges.

By fostering a growth mindset, encouraging effort and perseverance, and teaching self-compassion, you're giving your child the tools they need to build resilience and navigate life's inevitable ups and downs with grace and grit. Resilience is not just about surviving challenges; it's about thriving in the face of adversity.

Think about the times your child has faced a challenge and overcome it. Did they fall off their bike but get back on and try again? Did they struggle with a math concept but eventually master it with practice? These are everyday examples of resilience in action. Highlight these moments and celebrate their perseverance, reminding them of their ability to overcome obstacles.

As your child develops resilience, they'll not only bounce back from challenges but also approach social situations with more confidence and ease. These skills go hand in hand. In the next section, we'll explore some common hurdles elementary schoolers face – anxiety, bullies, peer pressure, academic struggles, and more. We'll equip you with strategies to help your child navigate these challenges and emerge stronger, with a greater sense of confidence and self-belief.

In Action: Building Bounce Back Ability 

✓ **The Budding Basketball Star:** Michael, a ten-year-old with dreams of NBA stardom, poured his heart into basketball. He practiced tirelessly, dribbling the ball around the house and honing his shooting skills at the local park. However, during an important game, Michael fumbled the ball, resulting in a turnover that led to the opposing team scoring the winning basket. Dejected and filled with self-doubt, Michael slumped on the bench, tears welling up in his eyes. His coach, recognizing his despair, knelt beside him and offered words of encouragement. He emphasized the importance of effort and perseverance, reminding Michael of all the hard work he had invested in his skills. The coach also pointed out that even the best players make mistakes, but it's how they respond that truly matters. Together, they developed a strategy to analyze Michael's performance and identify areas for improvement. With renewed determination and a growth mindset, Michael returned to practice the following week, his competitive spirit reignited.

Make it Happen: Learning Adventures 

✓ **Level Up Your Parenthood:**
  - **Focus on Effort and Progress:** Praise your child's effort and perseverance, not just the result.

- **Help Your Child Develop Coping Mechanisms:** Teach your child healthy coping mechanisms for dealing with stress and anxiety, such as deep breathing exercises, relaxation techniques, or mindfulness practices.
- **Model Resilience:** Be a role model for resilience by openly discussing your challenges and how you overcame them.
- **Provide Opportunities for Challenge:** Encourage your child to step outside their comfort zone and try new things, even if they feel scared or uncertain.

Navigating Common Hurdles: Anxiety, Bullies, Peer Pressure, Academic Struggles, and More

Elementary school is a time of incredible expansion for your child. They'll explore new subjects, forge deeper friendships, and discover hidden talents. It's like a thrilling expedition with uncharted territories to discover! But just like any adventure, there might be unexpected bumps along the road. As parents, you're their trusted guides, equipping them with the tools they need to navigate challenges and celebrate victories.

You might find yourself asking questions like: "Why does my child suddenly refuse to eat anything green?" "How can I help them make friends when they're so shy?" "When should I be concerned about my child's nightmares? These are all common concerns, and rest assured, you're not alone in facing them. In this section, we'll tackle these challenges head-on, providing practical strategies and compassionate guidance to empower you to help your child thrive.

Taming the Taste Bud Tantrum: A Guide to Elementary School Picky Eaters

Remember that fearless foodie who used to conquer every dish? They might now be waging war on vegetables, declaring broccoli and anything green to be the enemy. This sudden pickiness can be frustrating, but it's a normal part of growing up for elementary schoolers. Their taste buds are still maturing, and they might be more sensitive to flavors and textures than they were as little ones. On top of that, their friends' choices and their own growing independence can influence what they're willing to try.

The good news is, you can still guide them on a delicious journey towards healthy eating habits. Offer a colorful and diverse selection of healthy options at mealtimes. Let your child help with meal planning, or take them grocery shopping and allow them to pick out a new fruit or vegetable to explore each week. You can also get creative in the kitchen!

Experiment with fun recipes or turn food prep into a bonding experience – after all, who can resist a pizza topped with their favorite veggies?

Braver Than You Think: Helping Your Elementary Schooler Cope with Change

As your child's world expands to include school, friends, and new activities, separation anxiety might pop up again. It's less common than in toddlers or preschoolers, but can still occur, particularly in kindergarten or first grade, during times of change or stress, like starting a new school or dealing with family adjustments. It can be confusing for parents who think their child has "outgrown" separation anxiety. Rest assured, it's a normal reaction to new situations.

If your child seems clingy or anxious about being apart, reassure them of your love and support. Talk openly about their concerns and help them develop coping mechanisms. Practicing short separations, like spending an afternoon with a trusted friend or family member, can build confidence. Remind them of all the exciting things they'll do at school, and emphasize that you'll be waiting to pick them up with a big hug.

Sweet Dreams and Nighttime Fears

While nighttime awakenings and bad dreams may seem like a thing of the past for preschoolers, they can still be a common occurrence for elementary school children. Their imaginations are even more powerful now, and they might conjure up scary scenarios related to schoolwork, friendships, or even upcoming events.

The good news is that similar strategies used for preschoolers can still be effective in elementary school, with a slight twist. Here's how you can help your child achieve a restful night's sleep:

- **Establish a Consistent Routine:** Just like in preschool, a predictable bedtime routine signals to your child's body that it's time to wind down. Limit screen time before bed, as the blue light emitted from electronics disrupts sleep patterns.

- **Address Evolving Fears:** While monsters under the bed might have been a concern before, elementary schoolers might worry about upcoming tests, social interactions, or family changes. Talk openly about their concerns and provide reassurance.

- **Create a Calming Sleep Environment:** A dark, quiet, and cool bedroom promotes sleep. Consider using a nightlight if your child needs it, and create a relaxing atmosphere with calming bedtime stories or soothing music.

- **Comfort Nightmares:** If your child wakes up from a bad dream, comfort them, reassure them that they're safe, and help them get back to sleep. You can use the same techniques you might have used in preschool, like offering a hug or a favorite stuffed animal.

- **Consider a "Worry Box":** This strategy can still be helpful in elementary school. Encourage your child to write down their worries before bed, symbolically letting them go before sleep.

- **Seek Professional Help (if needed):** If nightmares persist or seem to be connected to a deeper emotional issue, consult your pediatrician to rule out any underlying medical or emotional problems.

Creating a predictable and calming bedtime routine can signal to your child's body that it's time to wind down. Limit screen time before bed, as the blue light emitted from electronic devices can interfere with sleep. If your child is struggling with specific fears, help them talk about their worries and offer reassurance.

Aggression and Bullying: Navigating Tricky Terrain

Aggression and bullying can be challenging behaviors to manage, but they're unfortunately not uncommon in elementary school. These behaviors often stem from frustration, lack of impulse control, or difficulty expressing needs. If your child is exhibiting aggressive behavior towards others, it's important to address the underlying causes. Talk to them about their feelings, teach them alternative ways to express anger or frustration, and model peaceful conflict resolution.

If your child is being bullied, listen to them without judgment, offer comfort and support, and work with their school to address the situation. Empower your child with strategies for dealing with bullies, such as walking away, telling an adult, or using humor to deflect insults. It's also important to help them build a strong sense of self-worth and confidence, as children who feel good about themselves are less likely to become targets of bullying. Teach them how to identify trusted adults at school and in their community who they can turn to for help.

Academic Anxiety and Struggles

The pressure to succeed in school can lead to academic anxiety and stress, which can manifest in physical symptoms like stomach aches and headaches, and emotional distress. Talk to your child about their worries, validate their feelings, and help them develop coping mechanisms. Encourage them to focus on their effort and progress rather than just grades, and remind them that you're proud of them no matter what.

If your child is struggling academically, work with their teacher to identify the specific areas of difficulty and develop a plan for support. This might involve extra help at school, tutoring, or exploring different learning styles. Encourage your child to ask for help when they need it, and celebrate their successes, no matter how small. Every child learns differently, and it's important to find strategies that work best for your child's individual needs and learning style.

Other Challenges: Navigating the Twists and Turns of Elementary School Life

Elementary school children are constantly growing and evolving, facing a variety of challenges beyond academics, friendships, and anxieties. Some children might struggle with adjusting to new routines, teachers, or classmates, while others might experience feelings of social exclusion or isolation. Extracurricular activities, while enriching, can also add pressure and create scheduling conflicts. Family changes, such as divorce, relocation, or the loss of a loved one, can also significantly affect your child's emotional well-being and performance at school.

I vividly remember when my own son, Ethan, started struggling with perfectionism in second grade. He was so focused on getting every answer right on his homework and tests that he became paralyzed by the fear of making mistakes. It was heartbreaking to see him so stressed and anxious. We started talking about the importance of learning from mistakes and celebrating effort over outcome. We also encouraged him to pursue activities he enjoyed purely for the fun of it, without the pressure of perfection. Slowly but surely, his anxiety eased, and he rediscovered the joy of learning.

It's important to remember that every child is unique, and their challenges will vary. Some children might be naturally resilient and adapt easily to change, while others might require more support and guidance. The key is to be patient, understanding, and supportive. Listen to your child's concerns without judgment, validate their feelings and offer reassurance and guidance. If you're unsure how to help your child, don't hesitate to seek support from their teachers, school counselors, or other professionals.

You're not alone in this journey. Millions of parents across the globe are facing similar challenges with their elementary school-aged children. By sharing experiences, seeking support, and equipping yourself with knowledge and tools, you can empower your child to thrive through this exciting and transformative phase of their lives.

As your child navigates the elementary years, remember that challenges are an inevitable part of growing up. These challenges, whether they involve anxiety, social struggles, academic pressures, or other hurdles, are not roadblocks but rather stepping stones on their path toward maturity and self-discovery. By equipping yourself with knowledge and a compassionate approach, you can guide your child through these trials, helping them develop the resilience and coping skills they need to thrive.

But elementary school is just one chapter in your child's ongoing journey. As they approach adolescence, a new set of challenges and opportunities await, accompanied by a whirlwind of physical, emotional, and social changes. In the next part, we'll transition into this exciting yet often turbulent phase, offering you a roadmap for understanding the teenage brain, strengthening communication, setting boundaries, and navigating the unique challenges of adolescence with empathy and understanding. We'll delve into topics like building strong communication, fostering positive connections with friends and family, navigating emotional challenges, and supporting your teenager's growing independence.

Mindful Parenting: Nurturing Strengths 

✓ **Pause & Reflect:**

- Think about your own childhood experiences in elementary school. Were there any specific challenges you faced? How did your parents help you navigate them?
- Think about any specific challenges your child is currently facing. What questions do you have? What resources could you explore to learn more and find support?
- What are some of your child's natural strengths and talents? How can you help them develop these further?
- How can you model healthy coping mechanisms for your child when dealing with challenges?

66

"We cannot make children learn. We can only provide them with the opportunity to do so."

\- MARIA MONTESSORI
(An Italian physician and educator)

Part 6:

Guiding Through Change: A Guide to Supporting Teenagers

Inside This Part

Take a deep breath, parents. We're venturing into a new frontier: the teenage years. It's a time of incredible growth and transformation, but also one that can be filled with eye rolls, slammed doors, and a whole lot of "I know, Mom/Dad!". If you're feeling a mix of excitement and apprehension, you're not alone. This is a time of change not just for your child, but for your relationship with them.

In this part, we're going to ditch the clichés about rebellious teens and moody adolescents. Instead, we'll dive into the science behind the teenage brain, offering a compassionate and understanding perspective on why they act the way they do. We'll explore how to navigate the often choppy waters of communication, setting boundaries that respect their growing independence while ensuring their safety and well-being.

But it's not all challenges. This is also a time of incredible potential, as your teenager discovers their passions, values, and unique identity. We'll talk about how to foster their self-esteem, encourage healthy risk-taking, and guide them towards making positive choices. We'll also tackle tough topics like academic stress, peer pressure, and social media influences, offering practical strategies for supporting your teen through these challenges. So, buckle up and get ready to embrace this exciting, sometimes bumpy, but ultimately rewarding journey through the teenage years.

The Teenage Brain: Embracing the Rollercoaster of Growth and Connection

Remember those early days when your child's brain was like a sponge, eagerly absorbing the world around them? Now, as you navigate the teenage years, it might feel like you're on an uncharted rollercoaster ride. Mood swings, perplexing choices, and a newfound reserve can leave you yearning for the open book your child once was.

But this phase of seeming disconnect is far from the end of your connection. In fact, it's a crucial period of growth and transformation, a time when your teenager's brain is undergoing a remarkable rewiring. It's like a bustling city under construction, with new neural pathways being forged, old ones pruned away, and connections strengthened. This overhaul is essential for their journey toward independence, but it can also lead to the turbulence we often associate with adolescence.

One of the most significant changes occurs in the prefrontal cortex, the brain's executive center responsible for decision-making, impulse control, and long-term planning. In teenagers, this "control tower" is still developing, which explains why they might struggle with impulsivity and have difficulty anticipating consequences.

Simultaneously, the limbic system, the brain's emotional center, is in overdrive. This surge of hormones fuels intense emotions, impulsive reactions, and a tendency to prioritize feelings over logic. It's like a car with a powerful engine but a wobbly steering wheel – lots of energy, but not always under control.

Beyond the emotional rollercoaster, these changes also affect social and emotional development. Teenagers become acutely aware of peer acceptance, yearn for social connection, and embark on a journey of self-discovery. They might question everything you've taught them, push boundaries and experiment with new identities. This can be challenging for parents, but it's a crucial part of their path toward finding their place in the world. Navigating this turbulent period requires understanding, patience, and a toolkit of strategies:

- **Embrace the Science:** Knowledge is empowering. Understanding the science behind the teenage brain promotes empathy and equips you to respond thoughtfully to their behavior.
- **Prioritize Connection:** Keep communication channels open, even when met with resistance. Be present, listen without judgment, and validate their emotions.
- **Set Clear Boundaries with Empathy:** While allowing space for exploration, maintain clear boundaries and expectations. This provides a sense of security during a time of change. Explain the "why" behind the rules, helping them understand the reasoning rather than feeling controlled.

- **Foster Independence:** Encourage decision-making within safe parameters. Allow them to experience natural consequences (within reason) and learn from their mistakes.
- **Nurture Emotional Intelligence:** Help your teen identify and express their emotions in healthy ways. Teach coping mechanisms for stress, anxiety, and anger.
- **Focus on Strengths:** Celebrate their achievements, encourage their passions, and foster a positive self-image. This builds resilience and confidence.
- **Be a Role Model:** Your actions speak volumes. Demonstrate healthy communication, emotional regulation, and problem-solving skills in your own life.

Parenting a teenager is a journey, not a destination. Seek support from other parents, educators, or therapists. This phase is temporary. With your love, guidance, and understanding, your teenager will emerge as a confident, capable, and independent young adult, ready to embrace the world with their unique gifts and passions.

In the next section, we'll delve into the art of building strong communication with your teenager. We'll explore how to create a safe space for open dialogue, practice respectful listening, and navigate challenging conversations with empathy and understanding.

In Action: Understanding the Teenage Brain 

✓ **The Tech Standoff:** John, a once chatty and affectionate 15-year-old, had become withdrawn and glued to his phone. Dinner conversations were punctuated by silence, and family game nights were a thing of the past. John's parents felt a growing disconnect and worried about his social isolation. Remembering what they had read about the teenage brain, they decided to approach the situation with empathy and understanding. John's father initiated a conversation, acknowledging John's passion for technology but also expressing a desire for more quality family time. Together, they brainstormed solutions, creating phone-free zones during meals and designating specific evenings for family activities. John, initially resistant, eventually appreciated the compromise. Family dinners became lively again, filled with conversation and laughter.

Navigating Identity: Maya, a bright and bubbly 14-year-old, had always excelled in school and extracurricular activities. Lately, however, she seemed unsure of herself, questioning her interests and spending hours browsing fashion websites. Her parents, used to her confident and outgoing personality, were concerned about this sudden shift. They reached out to Maya, creating a safe space for her to express her anxieties. By listening without judgment and validating her feelings, they learned that Maya was exploring different aspects of her identity and feeling pressure to fit in with a new group of friends. Together, they discussed the importance of staying true to herself while embracing new experiences. Maya joined a new art club, discovering a creative outlet and a community that embraced her individuality.

✓ Level Up Your Parenthood:

- **Schedule Regular Check-Ins:** Set aside dedicated time each week to connect with your teen, without distractions. This could be a car ride, a walk together, or an evening chat over a cup of tea.
- **Embrace Active Listening:** Practice active listening skills, giving your teen your full attention and validating their emotions. Avoid interrupting or offering unsolicited advice.
- **Focus on Interests:** Find common ground by engaging in activities your teen enjoys. This could be watching their favorite show, attending a sports game, or listening to their favorite music.
- **Open Communication is Key:** Encourage open communication by creating a safe space where your teen feels comfortable expressing their thoughts and feelings.
- **Celebrate Milestones:** Acknowledge and celebrate your teen's achievements, big or small. This reinforces positive behavior and builds their confidence.

Building Strong Communication: Open Dialogue and Respectful Listening

Imagine a bridge, connecting you and your teenager. It's not made of steel and concrete, but of words, feelings, and shared understanding. Building this bridge takes time and effort, but it's the most rewarding construction project you'll ever undertake.

Think back to the early days, when your child's coos and gurgles were their first attempts at communication. You responded with loving smiles and gentle words, fostering a sense of safety and connection. As they grew, their vocabulary expanded, and so did the depth of your conversations. Now, as teenagers, their thoughts and feelings are more complex, but the foundation you built – that open channel of communication – remains essential.

Open dialogue isn't just about talking; it's about creating a space where your teen feels safe to express themselves without fear of judgment or dismissal. Start by setting aside dedicated time for conversation, free from distractions. Put away your phones, turn off the TV, and truly be present. Ask open-ended questions that invite them to share their thoughts and feelings, such as, "What's been on your mind lately?" or "How are you feeling about school?"

Listening is the other half of the communication bridge. It means truly hearing what your teen is saying, not just waiting for your turn to speak. When they share, resist the urge to jump in with advice or solutions. Instead, validate their feelings with phrases like, "That sounds really tough" or "I understand why you're feeling that way."

Respectful listening also involves nonverbal cues. Make eye contact, nod your head, and use facial expressions to show you're engaged. Avoid interrupting or finishing their sentences. These small actions speak volumes about your willingness to understand their perspective.

Building a strong communication bridge isn't always smooth sailing. You'll encounter roadblocks like disagreements, misunderstandings, and even silence. That's okay. The key is to approach these challenges with patience and understanding.

If a conversation gets heated, take a break and come back to it later when everyone has cooled down. Be willing to apologize if you've made a mistake or spoken harshly. Most importantly, never give up on the bridge. Even if it feels like you're miles apart, keep reaching out, keep listening, and keep building. Here are a few additional tools for you to strengthen that bridge:

- **Find common ground:** Share interests and activities with your teen. This could be anything from watching a movie together to playing a game or trying a new hobby. Shared experiences create opportunities for bonding and conversation.
- **Show empathy:** Put yourself in your teen's shoes and try to see things from their perspective. This will help you respond with understanding and compassion, even when you don't agree with their choices.

- **Be a role model:** Demonstrate the kind of communication you want to see in your teen. Be open, honest, and respectful in your interactions.
- **Don't be afraid to seek help:** If you're struggling to connect with your teen, don't hesitate to reach out to a therapist or counselor. They can provide guidance and support to help you build a stronger relationship.

This bridge isn't just for your teenager. It's for you, too. It's a pathway to deeper connection, mutual respect, and a lifetime of shared understanding. Building this bridge may be a lifelong process, but the investment will yield invaluable returns in your relationship with your teen.

Open dialogue and respectful listening aren't just abstract concepts; they're the living, breathing foundations upon which healthy, thriving relationships are built. They are the tools that help us navigate the turbulent waters of adolescence and forge deeper connections with our teens. As we practice these skills, we'll find that the bridge we're building extends beyond our immediate family, shaping the way our teens interact with the world around them.

In the next section, we'll take the foundation we've built with open communication and respectful listening and apply it to the wider world our teens inhabit. We will delve into how these essential skills translate into healthy relationships of all kinds. We'll explore how setting clear boundaries, fostering mutual respect, and cultivating positive connections can empower teens to navigate the complexities of friendships, family dynamics, and even the budding landscape of romantic relationships. This journey will equip them with the tools they need to forge relationships that uplift and support them, not just now, but throughout their lives.

In Action: Building Bridges of Communication

✓ **The Silent Treatment:** Dinner at the Miller household had become a tense affair. Ever since Michael, a once chatty 16-year-old, had received a failing grade on his science project, a heavy silence hung in the air. His parents worried about his academic performance, and launched into a lecture about responsibility and hard work. Michael, feeling attacked and misunderstood, retreated behind a wall of silence, refusing to engage in conversation. Recognizing the growing disconnect, Michael's parents decided to try a different approach. The next evening, they set aside dedicated time for a conversation, putting away their phones and making eye contact. They used open-ended questions to understand Michael's perspective, acknowledging his frustration with the project and his fear of disappointing them. Michael, feeling heard and validated, opened up about the challenges he faced with the complex science concepts. Together, they brainstormed solutions, finding resources to help him understand the material and creating a plan to improve his study habits. This shift towards open dialogue and respectful listening not only addressed the academic issue but also strengthened their bond of trust and understanding.

Building Boundaries and Respect:
Fostering Positive Connections with Friends, Family, and Romantic Partners

The communication skills you've cultivated with your teen are like a compass, guiding them through the uncharted territory of friendships, family dynamics, and the first stirrings of romance. As a parent, you play a vital role in helping them interpret the map and navigate the twists and turns of these relationships.

Open the treasure chest of your own experiences. Share tales of your teenage friendships – the inside jokes, the shared dreams, the inevitable fallouts and reconciliations. Tell them about your first crush, the butterflies in your stomach, the awkward moments, and the lessons learned. By sharing your vulnerabilities and triumphs, you normalize the rollercoaster of emotions that comes with relationships. This not only deepens your connection with your teen but also shows them that they are not alone in their struggles.

Explain to your teen that relationships are like a well-choreographed dance, where each partner takes turns leading and following. It's a delicate balance of self-expression and attentive listening, of asserting needs while respecting the boundaries of others. Encourage them to ask themselves:

- **"Am I truly listening to what my friend/partner/family member is saying, or am I just waiting for my turn to talk?"**
- **"Am I expressing my needs and desires clearly, but also respecting the other person's right to have different opinions or feelings?"**
- **"Am I willing to compromise and find solutions that work for both of us?"**

As your teen ventures deeper into the social world, they'll inevitably encounter peer pressure. Peer pressure can be a powerful force, especially during adolescence. Talk openly about its subtle and not-so-subtle forms, from the fear of missing out (FOMO) to the pressure to conform to certain styles or behaviors. Help your teen develop a strong internal compass, guided by their values, beliefs, and passions. Give them practical tools for resisting negative peer pressure, such as:

- **Reframing the Situation:** Instead of seeing it as a rejection, encourage them to view saying "no" as an act of self-respect.
- **The Power of "I":** Help them practice assertive statements like "I don't feel comfortable with that" or "I'd rather not."
- **Finding Their Tribe:** Encourage them to seek out friends who share their values and interests, creating a supportive network that celebrates individuality.

Family Dynamics: A Laboratory for Healthy Conflict Resolution

Family relationships are a microcosm of the wider world, a place where your teen can learn and practice essential skills for navigating conflict and building strong bonds. Encourage them to view disagreements as opportunities for growth, rather than battles to be won. Model healthy conflict resolution by:

- **Active Listening:** Giving your full attention to the person speaking, without interrupting or judging.
- **Expressing Feelings Respectfully:** Using "I" statements to express how you feel, rather than blaming or accusing others.
- **Seeking Win-Win Solutions:** Brainstorming creative ways to address the issue that satisfies everyone's needs as much as possible.

By fostering a culture of open communication and respectful disagreement within your family, you're giving your teen a valuable gift — the ability to navigate conflict with grace and emerge from it with stronger relationships.

Romantic Relationships: The Dance of Respect and Self-Discovery

As your teen dips their toes into the waters of romance, it's essential to have candid conversations about what constitutes a healthy relationship. Discuss the importance of:

- **Mutual Respect:** Partners should value each other's opinions, feelings, and boundaries.
- **Open Communication:** Talking openly and honestly about both the joys and challenges of the relationship.
- **Consent:** Understanding that consent is a clear, enthusiastic "yes" and that it can be withdrawn at any time.
- **Individuality:** Maintaining one's own interests, hobbies, and friendships is crucial for a healthy relationship.

Help your teen understand that love should never come at the cost of their self-respect or well-being. Encourage them to choose partners who lift them up, not tear them down.

Building Strong Bonds: Communication, Boundaries, and Respect in Teen Relationships

Boundaries are not about building walls but about creating healthy guidelines for all relationships. Help teens identify physical, emotional and digital boundaries. Encourage them to communicate these boundaries clearly and assertively, using phrases like:

- **"I need some space right now."**
- **"I'm not comfortable with that."**
- **"Please respect my privacy."**

Remind them that it's okay to say "no" to anything that makes them feel uncomfortable or unsafe, and that true friends and partners will respect their decisions.

By equipping your teen with these essential tools for building healthy relationships, you're not just preparing them for the teenage years; you're setting them up for a lifetime of fulfilling and meaningful connections. This is a journey you take together, one filled with open conversations, mutual respect, and unwavering love.

As your teen navigates the maze of relationships, armed with the tools of communication, respect, and boundary-setting, they're not just building connections with others – they're also strengthening their relationship with themselves. Each interaction, each decision, each moment of self-advocacy contributes to a growing sense of self-worth and confidence.

This journey of self-discovery is a vital part of adolescence, and as parents, we have the privilege of witnessing and supporting it. In the next section, we'll delve into how you can empower your teenager to embrace their unique strengths and navigate the inevitable self-doubt that comes with growing up. Together, we'll explore strategies for fostering self-acceptance, building resilience, and cultivating the kind of unshakeable confidence that will carry them through life's challenges.

Mindful Parenting: Building Bridges of Trust 

✓ **Pause & Reflect:**

- Consider your teenage years. What were some of the challenges you faced in your relationships with friends, family, and romantic partners? How can you use those experiences to guide your teen?
- Do you feel comfortable communicating openly with your teen about sensitive topics like relationships, peer pressure, and consent? If not, what steps can you take to create a safer space for conversation?
- Think about a recent conflict you had with your teen. What went well? What could have been handled differently?

From Self-Doubt to Self-Acceptance: *Empowering Your Teenager with Confidence*

As your teenager navigates the maze of adolescence, their inner landscape is undergoing its own transformation. Amidst the physical changes and newfound independence, a battle often rages within—the battle between self-doubt and self-acceptance.

Just like a butterfly emerging from its chrysalis, your teen is unfolding into their true self, yet doubts and insecurities can cloud their wings. It's a natural part of growing up, a universal experience we've all encountered. But as parents, you have the power to be the steady hand that guides them through this challenging yet crucial phase.

Your teen might grapple with questions like "Do I fit in?" "Am I good enough?" or "What am I passionate about?" These are the questions that shape their identity and self-perception. And while it's tempting to rush in with ready-made answers or dismiss their worries as "just teenage angst," remember that this is their journey, not yours. Your role is to create a safe and supportive space where they can explore these questions for themselves, without judgment or pressure.

Self-acceptance is a lifelong journey, but the seeds are often sown during adolescence. Here are some ways you can help your teen cultivate a healthy sense of self:

- **Celebrate their uniqueness:** Encourage them to embrace their quirks, passions, and talents. Help them see that what makes them different is what makes them special. If they love anime, celebrate it! If they're passionate about coding, support their endeavors.

- **Focus on effort, not just outcomes:** Praise their hard work and perseverance, even if they don't always achieve the desired result. Did they study hard for a test but didn't get the grade they hoped for? Acknowledge their effort and help them see what they can learn from the experience. This helps them develop a growth mindset, where they see challenges as opportunities for learning and improvement.

- **Be their safe haven:** Let your teen know that they can always come to you with their doubts and fears, without fear of judgment or criticism. Listen with empathy and offer unconditional love and support. Sometimes, all they need is a shoulder to cry on or a listening ear.

- **Mirror back their strengths:** Help them recognize and appreciate their positive qualities. Point out their kindness, creativity, intelligence, or resilience. For example, "I was so impressed by how you handled that disagreement with your friend. You were so calm and respectful."

- **Challenge negative self-talk:** When you hear your teen engaging in negative self-talk, gently challenge those thoughts. Help them reframe their perspective and focus on their strengths. For instance, if they say, "I'm so dumb, I failed that test," you might respond, "You're not dumb, you just had a tough time with that particular subject. Remember how well you did in your history project?"

Self-acceptance is not about being perfect. It's about recognizing and appreciating all aspects of oneself—the strengths, the weaknesses, the light, and the shadow. It's about embracing the journey of self-discovery, with all its twists and turns, and realizing that true confidence comes from within, not from external validation.

As your teen develops a stronger sense of self-acceptance, they'll be better equipped to handle the challenges and uncertainties that life throws their way. They'll be more resilient, more confident, and more empowered to chase their dreams and live a life that's true to themselves. This journey is not always easy, but with your love, support, and guidance, your teen can emerge from adolescence with a solid foundation of self-worth that will serve them well throughout their lives.

Teens often grapple with conflicting emotions as they discover who they are. Self-doubt can battle with newfound confidence, and anxieties about fitting in can clash with a desire for individuality. This emotional rollercoaster is a normal part of adolescence. However, open communication with your teen can be a powerful tool. By creating a safe space for them to express their feelings, fears, and dreams, you can help them navigate this journey of self-discovery. Sharing your own experiences with self-doubt and insecurity can also be helpful. It shows your teen that they're not alone and that everyone faces challenges in finding their place in the world.

In the next section, we'll delve into the tools and strategies that can help your teen weather the emotional ups and downs of adolescence. We'll explore how to foster resilience, manage stress, and develop the emotional intelligence needed to navigate the complex landscape of adulthood. Together, we'll empower your teen to embrace their emotions as valuable messengers, guiding them towards a fulfilling and meaningful life.

In Action: Cultivating Self-Acceptance 

- **The Struggling Artist:** David, a shy and introverted 16-year-old, harbored a deep passion for art. He poured his emotions onto the canvas, his artwork bursting with vibrant colors and raw expression. However, David's self-doubt held him back. He constantly compared his work to other artists online, feeling his own creations fell short. One day, while cleaning his room, David's mother stumbled upon a hidden portfolio filled with his artwork. Impressed by his talent and recognizing his self-criticism, she encouraged him to showcase his work in the upcoming school art fair. David was hesitant at first, his self-doubt whispering negativity. However, with his mother's gentle support and encouragement to focus on his own unique artistic voice, David decided to take a leap of faith. The art fair was a success, with many admiring his work. This positive experience boosted David's confidence, and he began to appreciate his own artistic talents.

- **The Friendship Fallout:** Maya, a social butterfly, thrived on positive attention from her friends. Her sense of self-worth was often tied to external validation. When a misunderstanding led to a falling out with her closest friend group, Maya's world came crashing down. Feeling isolated and rejected, she questioned her self-worth and retreated into her shell. Her parents, aware of her dependence on external validation, decided to help her cultivate a stronger sense of self-acceptance. They encouraged her to reconnect with activities she enjoyed outside of the friend group, such as playing the guitar and volunteering at the animal shelter. They also helped her identify her positive qualities, reminding her of her kindness, creativity, and resilience. As Maya reconnected with her passions and rediscovered her inner strength, she began to feel more complete within herself, less reliant on external validation for her sense of self-worth.

Navigating Emotional Challenges and Fostering Independence:
Building Resilience, Managing Stress, and Preparing for Adulthood

Imagine your teen as a majestic tall ship, setting sail on the vast and often unpredictable ocean of adolescence. The winds may change, storms may brew, and the waves of peer pressure and societal expectations may rise and fall. But with your guidance, they can learn to navigate these turbulent waters with confidence and resilience.

Think of emotional resilience as the anchor that keeps the ship steady amidst life's tempests. It's not about avoiding rough seas altogether, but rather developing the strength to weather them. As a parent, you are the lighthouse, casting a steady beam of support and guidance through the darkness. Encourage your teen to share their struggles, and to talk about the fears and anxieties that keep them up at night. Validate their emotions, reminding them that it's okay to feel overwhelmed or uncertain.

Just like a ship has tools for navigating choppy waters, your teen can learn to navigate emotional challenges with healthy coping mechanisms. But remember, they might not always know where to find these tools. It's your job to introduce them to different stress-management techniques, such as:

- **Deep breathing exercises:** Simple techniques like box breathing (inhale for 4 counts, hold for 4 counts, exhale for 4 counts, hold for 4 counts) can calm the nervous system and reduce anxiety.
- **Mindfulness practices:** Encourage your teen to focus on the present moment, without judgment. This can help them tune out their worries and become more aware of their emotions.
- **Physical activity:** Exercise is a natural stress reliever, releasing endorphins that boost mood and reduce tension.
- **Creative expression:** Activities like drawing, writing, or playing music can be therapeutic outlets for emotions.

- **Connecting with nature:** Spending time outdoors has been shown to reduce stress, improve mood, and boost creativity.

Setbacks are not failures, but opportunities for growth. Share stories of your challenges and how you learned from them. Did you ever fail a test, get rejected from a job, or experience heartbreak? Your teen can learn valuable lessons from your experiences. Help them reframe their perspective, viewing mistakes as stepping stones on their path to success. Cultivate a growth mindset, where they see challenges as a chance to learn and develop new skills. Resilience is not about never falling, but about getting back up stronger.

As your teen's journey continues, they'll yearn for more autonomy and independence. Think of this as them taking the helm of their own ship, charting a course toward their unique destination. As a parent, this can be exciting and terrifying. But remember, your goal is not to control their journey but to equip them with the skills and confidence to navigate it on their own.

Gradually loosen the reins, entrusting them with age-appropriate responsibilities, such as managing their own schedule, making decisions about their extracurricular activities, or even taking on a part-time job. Celebrate their successes and be their sounding board when they face difficult choices. Offer guidance and support, but also give them the space to make their own mistakes and learn from them. Trust that you've equipped them with the tools they need to navigate life's challenges. In this way, you're not just preparing them for adulthood; you're empowering them to become confident, resilient, and capable captains of their own lives, ready to explore the vast ocean of possibilities that lie ahead.

By fostering emotional resilience, teaching stress management skills, and gradually granting them independence, you're giving your teen the most valuable gift of all: the ability to navigate life's storms with confidence, grace, and a sense of purpose. Your role is not to shield them from all adversity but to equip them with the tools they need to face it head-on. And as they set sail on this exciting journey of self-discovery, you'll be there to cheer them on, offer guidance when needed, and celebrate their victories every step of the way.

In the next section, we'll delve into these specific challenges, equipping you with the knowledge and strategies to support your teen as they navigate academic stress, the lure of substance abuse, the complexities of peer pressure, and the ever-present influence of social media. We'll explore how to open up conversations about these sensitive topics, offer guidance without judgment, and help your teen make informed decisions that align with their values and goals.

In Action: Building Emotional Resilience 

- ✓ **The Test Anxiety Triumph:** Erica, a bright and ambitious 15-year-old, battled with crippling test anxiety. The pressure to succeed often left her feeling overwhelmed and paralyzed. Leading up to a major exam, she experienced physical symptoms like nausea and difficulty concentrating. Her parents, recognizing her anxiety, decided to help her develop healthy coping mechanisms. They introduced her to relaxation techniques like deep breathing exercises and guided meditation. They encouraged her to create a dedicated study space free from distractions and helped her develop a realistic study schedule to manage her workload. On the day of the exam,

Erica practiced her deep breathing exercises and used positive affirmations to calm her nerves. The result? While still nervous, she felt more in control and was able to focus on her knowledge. Erica's success story boosted her confidence, and she continued to utilize these coping mechanisms to manage stress in other areas of her life.

Specific Challenges: *Academic Stress, Substance Abuse, Navigating Peer Pressure, and Social Media Influences*

The teenage years are like a thrilling roller coaster ride, filled with exhilarating highs and stomach-churning lows. As your teen navigates this uncharted territory, they'll encounter unique challenges that can test their newfound resilience and independence. Think of these challenges as unexpected twists and turns in the track, each one an opportunity for growth and learning.

One of the most common hurdles teens face is academic stress. The pressure to excel in school, get good grades, and make important decisions about their future can feel like a heavy backpack weighing them down. As a parent, you can lighten their load by creating a supportive and encouraging home environment. Imagine a cozy study nook with good lighting and a comfortable chair, where they can focus on their schoolwork without distractions. Offer help when needed, but also respect their growing autonomy by allowing them to take ownership of their studies.

Your teen isn't just a student; they're a whole person with diverse interests and passions. Encourage them to explore activities outside of school that bring them joy and help them de-stress. Whether it's playing a sport, joining a club, or simply spending time with friends, these outlets can provide a much-needed balance and perspective. Help them discover what recharges their batteries and makes them feel alive, and encourage them to prioritize those activities. Not only will this help them manage stress, but it will also promote a sense of well-roundedness and self-discovery.

Substance Abuse: A Conversation, Not a Confrontation

As your teen navigates the social landscape of adolescence, they may encounter the allure of substance abuse. It's important to have open and honest conversations about the risks associated with drugs and alcohol.

It's normal to be curious about substances as you explore the world around you. Let your teen know you're open to discussing it honestly without judgment. This creates a safe space for them to express their questions and concerns.

Provide factual information about the dangers of drug and alcohol use. Explain the immediate and long-term health risks relevant to their age group. This could include impaired judgment, coordination problems, addiction, and long-term health problems.

Approach the conversation with curiosity and empathy. Listen to your teen's concerns and questions without judgment. Understanding their motivations is key. Is it peer pressure, a desire to fit in, or an attempt to cope with stress, anxiety, or boredom?

If your teen opens up about experimenting with substances, resist the urge to panic or punish. Instead, focus on understanding the underlying issues and help them develop healthier coping mechanisms. Discuss alternative ways to manage stress, anxiety, or boredom. This could include exercise, spending time with positive friends, exploring new hobbies, or relaxation techniques.

Seek professional guidance if needed. Remember, your unwavering support can be a powerful factor in their decision to make healthy choices. Let them know you're there for them and that you'll support them in seeking help if they need it.

Peer Pressure: Finding Their Inner Compass

Imagine your teen at a party, a cacophony of loud music and laughter swirling around them. A group of friends approaches, offering something that clashes with their gut feeling. The pressure to be accepted, to be part of the group, can be overwhelming. But how can you equip them to navigate these situations and discover their own unique compass?

Resisting negative peer pressure starts with self-awareness. Help your teen identify their core values and the guiding principles that shape their choices. Is honesty their north star? Do kindness and respect light their path? Explore these values together, discussing how their actions can reflect them. Encourage them to explore interests and passions – shared activities can connect them with like-minded peers who share their values, creating a natural support system.

Saying "no" can feel like climbing a wall, but assertive communication is the key. Role-play different scenarios where your teen might face peer pressure. Practice ways for them to decline confidently, without resorting to rudeness. Phrases like "Thanks, but I'm not interested" or "That's not really my scene" can be effective. Encourage them to suggest alternatives or simply excuse themselves from the situation.

Peer pressure isn't always the enemy. Positive influences can motivate your teen to try new things, push their boundaries, or even excel in academics or sports. Talk about the difference between healthy encouragement and negative pressure to conform.

Social media can be another battleground for peer pressure. Discuss how online trends or group chats can create pressure to participate in risky behavior. Talk about responsible digital citizenship and how to be a positive influence online. Encourage them to curate their online experience, follow accounts that uplift and inspire them, and speak out against negativity or cyberbullying.

By fostering open communication and critical thinking skills, you can equip your teen to navigate peer pressure with confidence. Help them develop a strong sense of self, surround themselves with positive influences, and make choices that align with their values, both online and offline. Remember, they don't have to weather this storm alone. You are their anchor, their guiding light, and their biggest supporter on this journey of self-discovery.

Social Media: A Launchpad for Connection, or a Rabbit Hole of Comparison?

In today's world, social media is an undeniable force in teenagers' lives. It offers a vibrant platform for connection, self-expression, and exploration. They can connect with friends, discover new interests, and share their passions with the world. However, this digital landscape can also be a double-edged sword. While it fosters connection, it can also fuel feelings of anxiety, inadequacy, and isolation.

Unfortunately, the positive aspects of social media can be overshadowed by the dangers of cyberbullying. Teens are bombarded with carefully curated online personas, often leading to social comparison and a distorted sense of reality.

This relentless pressure to achieve an unrealistic ideal can be detrimental to their self-esteem.

So, how can you empower your teen to navigate this complex digital world? Here's how you can embark on this journey together:

- **Become Cyber Savvy:** Equip your teen with the knowledge to recognize the red flags of cyberbullying. Discuss the different forms it can take, from the sting of online name-calling to the invisibility caused by deliberate exclusion. Talk openly about the relentless negativity of online harassment and its damaging effects.
- **Develop a Response Plan:** Knowledge is power, but knowing how to respond is just as crucial. Role-play different cyberbullying scenarios together. Help your teen develop calm and assertive

responses that cut off negativity at the source. Blocking bullies is a powerful first step, but don't forget the importance of reporting incidents to you or another trusted adult. Remember, they are not alone in facing these challenges.

- **Be a Force for Good:** Being a responsible digital citizen goes beyond personal protection. Teens have the power to be positive forces online. Discuss the importance of bystander intervention. If your teen witnesses cyberbullying, encourage them to report the incident and offer support to the victim. A simple act of kindness, like a message of encouragement, can make a world of difference.

By fostering open communication and critical thinking skills, you can equip your teen to be not just safe, but also a positive influence online. Together, you can help them navigate the social media landscape with resilience, the confidence to stand up for themselves and others, and the self-awareness to curate a digital experience that uplifts and empowers them.

Empower your teen to be a positive force online, navigating the digital world with confidence and self-awareness.

Your Role as a Guide and Advocate

You're not alone in this journey. Many resources are available to help you and your teen navigate these challenges. School counselors, therapists, and online resources can offer valuable guidance and support. Feel free to contact them if you need help. By working together, you can empower your teen to make wise choices, build resilience, and emerge from adolescence with a strong sense of self and a bright future ahead. You are their most important ally and advocate. Your love, guidance, and unwavering support will make all the difference in their journey towards adulthood.

As your teen navigates the complexities of adolescence and faces these unique challenges, it's important to remember that your own journey as a parent is equally transformative. In the next part, we'll shift our focus to how the act of raising children can shape and change us in unexpected ways, revealing hidden strengths and newfound depths of compassion. Get ready to explore the gifts of growth that parenthood brings, the lessons you learn from your children, and the profound ways they change your perspective on life.

In Action: Navigating Challenges

✓ **The Social Media Savvy Stand:** David, a kind and empathetic 15-year-old, witnessed a classmate being cyberbullied on social media. The relentless online taunts and exclusion left the victim feeling isolated and ostracized. David, remembering conversations with his parents about responsible digital citizenship, decided to act. He didn't engage with the bullies directly, but instead, offered support to the victim through a private message. He also contacted a trusted adult, informing them about the situation. With his parents' guidance, David reported the cyberbullying to the social media platform. His act of courage not only helped the victim but also empowered other classmates to stand up against online negativity. This experience solidified David's belief in using social media for good and the importance of being a positive force online.

Make it Happen: Setting Goals and Building Support 

✓ **Level Up Your Parenthood:**

- **Lead by Example:** Practice healthy coping mechanisms for stress management in your own life. Teens are keen observers, and your approach to challenges will influence theirs.

- **Set Realistic Expectations:** Work with your teen to establish realistic academic goals. Focus on effort, progress, and a growth mindset over the pressure to achieve perfection.

- **Monitor Social Media Use:** Discuss healthy boundaries for social media use. Set time limits and encourage your teen to curate their online experience, following positive and uplifting content.

- **Develop a Support System:** Help your teen build a strong support system beyond their immediate family. Encourage them to connect with positive friends, mentors, or school counselors who can offer guidance and encouragement.

> **"You are your child's first and most important role model."**

- W. TIMOTHY MOUSSEAU
(An American author and fatherhood speaker)

Part 7:

The Gift of Growth: How Parenthood Changes You

Inside This Part

Parenting, much like childhood, is a journey of growth, learning, and transformation. It's a wild ride that can test your limits, push you out of your comfort zone, and ultimately, reveal the incredible capacity of the human heart. While we often focus on the ways we shape our children's lives, it's equally important to acknowledge how our children shape us.

In this part, we'll delve into the unexpected gifts of parenthood, the ways in which raising children can transform our own lives. We'll explore how the daily challenges and triumphs of parenting can cultivate patience, resilience, empathy, and a renewed sense of wonder. We'll learn how our children can become our greatest teachers, showing us how to slow down, appreciate the small moments, and find joy in the simple things.

Whether you're a new parent navigating sleepless nights and endless diaper changes or a seasoned pro juggling the complexities of raising teenagers, this part is for you. It's an invitation to reflect on your own journey of growth and to celebrate the incredible ways in which parenthood has enriched your life.

From "Hurry Up!" to "I Can Wait": Cultivating Patience and Empathy on the Parenting Journey

Remember those frantic mornings, racing against the clock to get everyone out the door? Shoes MIA, spilled cereal turning the kitchen floor into a sticky obstacle course, and the relentless ticking of the clock threatening to derail your carefully planned schedule. In those moments, it's easy to resort to that familiar refrain: "Hurry up!"

But what if we told you that parenthood has a secret superpower, one that can transform those harried mornings into opportunities for connection and growth? That superpower is patience, the ability to pause, breathe, and respond with understanding rather than react with frustration.

Now, before you roll your eyes and think, "Easier said than done," hear us out. We know that patience isn't always easy, especially when you're juggling a million tasks and your toddler is gleefully dumping their juice cup on the carpet. But here's the thing: patience isn't just about gritting your teeth and enduring the chaos. It's about shifting your perspective, slowing down your own internal clock, and seeing the world through your child's eyes.

Imagine, for a moment, that you're a tiny explorer, navigating a world full of fascinating sights, sounds, and textures. Every object is a potential adventure, every task an opportunity for learning and discovery. Suddenly, that spilled cereal becomes a sensory experiment, the missing shoe a chance to practice problem-solving skills.

When we approach parenting with patience and empathy, we create space for our children to grow and learn at their own pace. We allow them to experience the world with wonder and curiosity, unhurried by our own anxieties and expectations. And in the process, we ourselves become more patient, more understanding, and more present.

So next time you find yourself on the verge of shouting "Hurry up!" take a deep breath and remember the power of patience. Step into your child's shoes, see the world through their eyes and allow yourself to be swept away by their boundless enthusiasm and curiosity. You might just find that those moments of chaos become cherished memories and that the journey of parenthood is a lot more enjoyable when you slow down and savor the ride. But how do we cultivate this elusive patience?

- **Start with self-compassion:** You're human. It's okay to feel frustrated or overwhelmed at times. Acknowledge your emotions and give yourself grace. Parenting is hard, and it's okay to not be perfect.
- **Practice mindfulness:** Take a few moments each day to simply be present with your child, without judgment or agenda. Notice their expressions, their movements, their joy in the mundane. This can

help you connect with their experience and see the world from their perspective.

- **Find your zen:** Discover calming practices that work for you, whether it's deep breathing, yoga, meditation, or simply taking a walk in nature. Having a go-to relaxation technique can help you de-stress in the moment and build your overall capacity for patience.

- **Choose your battles:** Not every spilled cup or missed deadline is worth getting upset over. Save your energy for the things that truly matter, like teaching your child valuable life skills and fostering a loving connection.

- **Focus on connection:** When you feel your patience wearing thin, remember that your child's behavior is often a way of communicating their needs. Take a moment to connect with them, offer a hug, or simply listen to their perspective. This can help you understand what's driving their behavior and respond with empathy rather than anger.

- **Practice proactive patience:** Anticipate potential triggers for impatience, such as rushed mornings or transitions between activities. Plan ahead to minimize stress and build in extra time for your child to adjust.

Patience isn't a finish line you cross, but an ongoing journey. Some days will be easier than others, but with practice and intention, you can cultivate this superpower and transform your parenting experience. Not only will your child benefit from your calm and loving presence, but you'll also discover a deeper sense of peace and joy amidst the beautiful chaos.

As you embrace the power of patience and empathy, you'll discover a profound transformation within yourself. The challenges of parenting, the moments that test your patience and push you to your limits, can also become unexpected catalysts for growth, revealing a strength you never knew you possessed.

In the next chapter, we'll dive deeper into this metamorphosis, exploring how the journey of parenthood can shape you into a stronger, more resilient, and ultimately, more fearless individual. You may be surprised to discover the hidden depths of your courage, the resilience you didn't know you had, and the remarkable ways in which parenting can empower you to face your own fears and insecurities head-on.

In Action: Navigating Challenges

- **The Meltdown in the Cereal Aisle:** Emily, a busy working mom, found her mornings a constant battle against the clock. One particularly hectic day, she rushed her son, Ethan, through the grocery store. His pleas to linger by the toy aisle met with a hurried "No, we don't have time." Finally reaching the cereal section, Ethan threw a full-blown tantrum, scattering boxes and flinging himself to the ground. Emily, overwhelmed and on the verge of tears herself, felt a surge of impatience. However, remembering her recent commitment to cultivating patience, she took a deep breath. Squatting down to Ethan's eye level, she acknowledged his frustration and offered him a choice of two cereals. Ethan, feeling heard and empowered, calmed down instantly, selecting a cereal and even helping to restock the fallen boxes. This experience highlighted the importance of empathy and recognizing the emotional needs behind children's behavior.

- **The Patience Pays Off:** David, a first-time dad, struggled with his daughter Lily's seemingly endless stream of questions.

"Why is the sky blue?" "Where do clouds go at night?" His initial response was often a dismissive "I don't know, honey, can we talk about this later?" However, after reading about the importance of patience in fostering a child's curiosity, he decided to shift his approach. The next time Lily bombarded him with questions, he took a deep breath and adopted a more patient demeanor. He knelt down to her level, making eye contact, and offered genuine answers, even when he didn't have all the solutions. Lily's face lit up with delight, andtheir conversations became a cherished bonding experience. David discovered that patience wasn't just about waiting, but about creating space for exploration and learning.

From Fragile to Fearless: *Discovering Your Inner Strength as a Parent*

Remember that moment you first held your child in your arms? The world tilted on its axis, and a wave of fierce protectiveness washed over you. You felt a surge of love so intense, so unconditional, that it took your breath away. In that instant, you might have felt both incredibly strong and incredibly vulnerable – a paradox that lies at the heart of parenthood.

The truth is, that parenting is a journey that tests our limits, stretches our boundaries, and pushes us to confront our deepest fears. It can leave us feeling exposed, uncertain, and at times, completely overwhelmed. But within these very challenges lies the potential for incredible personal growth.

Think about it: raising a child requires a level of courage that you may not have even known you possessed. The sleepless nights, the endless worries, the constant juggling of responsibilities – it all takes a tremendous amount of inner strength. Each time you soothe a crying baby, face a defiant toddler or support a heartbroken teenager, you're tapping into a well of resilience that might have been hidden beneath the surface. Every hurdle you overcome as a parent strengthens your resolve and builds your confidence in your own abilities.

Parenthood can also awaken a newfound sense of purpose and clarity. The sheer intensity of loving another human being so deeply can shift your priorities, reframe your values, and give your life a renewed sense of meaning. You might find yourself letting go of old habits, embracing new passions, and redefining what truly matters. Perhaps you discover a hidden talent for storytelling as you invent bedtime tales, or maybe you find a newfound appreciation for nature as you explore the world with your child.

And as you navigate the ups and downs of parenting, you'll discover that your capacity for empathy and compassion expands exponentially. You'll learn to see the world through your child's eyes, to understand their struggles, and to celebrate their triumphs with unbridled joy. This deeper understanding of the human experience can ripple out into all areas of your life, enriching your relationships with your partner, family, friends, and even strangers. You may find yourself more patient, more understanding, and more forgiving, both with yourself and with others.

So, while parenting may initially feel like a fragile dance, a delicate balancing act of love and fear, it can also be a catalyst for incredible transformation. It can empower you to step out of your comfort zone, face your vulnerabilities, and discover a strength you never knew you had. As you embrace the challenges and joys of parenthood, you'll find that you are not just raising a child; you're also raising a stronger, braver, and more compassionate version of yourself. As you navigate the ever-changing landscape of parenthood, embrace these key principles to foster your own growth alongside your child's:

- **Parenting is a mirror:** Your child's behavior can often reflect your own strengths and weaknesses. Use these moments as opportunities for self-reflection and growth. When your child throws a tantrum, instead of reacting with anger, ask yourself: What might be triggering this behavior? Am I modeling healthy emotional regulation?
- **Embrace the imperfections:** Don't strive for perfection; aim for progress. Every mistake is a chance to learn and become a better parent. It's okay to apologize to your child when you've messed up. This teaches them humility and forgiveness.
- **Celebrate your wins:** Acknowledge your accomplishments, both big and small. You're doing an amazing job! Parenting is hard work, and it's important to give yourself credit for the effort you put in.

- **Ask for help when you need it:** There's no shame in seeking support from your partner, family, friends, or professionals. We all need a helping hand sometimes. Whether it's a listening ear, a shoulder to cry on, or practical advice, reaching out for help can make all the difference.

The journey of parenthood is an ongoing adventure, full of surprises, challenges, and rewards. By embracing the growth and transformation that comes with it, you'll not only become a better parent but also a more empowered, resilient, and compassionate human being. You may discover hidden talents, passions, and strengths you never knew you had. The experience of raising a child can unlock new dimensions of your personality and open your heart to a deeper understanding of the world and yourself.

So, embrace the challenges, the triumphs, and the beautiful messiness of parenthood. Allow yourself to be transformed by this incredible journey. Your strength as a parent is not just about weathering the storms; it's about discovering the unwavering light that shines within you, illuminating the path for both you and your child.

In the next chapter, we'll explore another extraordinary gift of parenthood: the ability to see the world anew through the wonder-filled eyes of your child. Prepare to rediscover the magic of everyday moments, the joy of simple pleasures, and the boundless curiosity that makes life an endless adventure.

Make it Happen: Cultivating Calm & Confidence 

✓ Level Up Your Parenthood:
- **Embrace Self-Reflection:** Take time for regular self-

reflection. Journal about your experiences, identify areas for growth and celebrate your accomplishments.

- **Practice Mindfulness:** Mindfulness exercises like meditation or deep breathing can help you manage stress and cultivate emotional awareness.
- **Connect with Other Parents:** Build a support network of other parents who can offer encouragement, advice, and a listening ear.
- **Strengthen Your Relationship with Your Partner:** Prioritize quality time with your partner. A strong support system at home is essential for navigating the challenges of parenthood.
- **Practice Self-Care:** Don't neglect your own needs. Schedule time for activities that bring you joy and relaxation.

The World Through Wonder-Filled Eyes: *Seeing Life Anew Through Your Child's Lens*

Remember the last time your child pointed out a ladybug on a leaf, their eyes sparkling with wonder? Or the way they marveled at a rainbow arcing across the sky, their face alight with pure joy? Children possess an almost magical ability to find magic in the mundane, to see the world with fresh eyes, unburdened by the cynicism and jadedness that can often accompany adulthood. Their boundless curiosity and infectious enthusiasm can be a breath of fresh air for us as parents, reminding us of the simple pleasures we may have overlooked in our busy lives.

As parents, we have the incredible opportunity to rediscover this sense of wonder through our children. By slowing down, paying attention, and truly being present with them, we can tap into the simple joys that often get lost in the hustle and bustle of daily life. Instead of rushing from one task to the next, pause to watch your child play. Notice the way they examine a flower petal with delicate fascination, the way they giggle at a silly joke that tickles their soul, or the way they marvel at the moon and stars, their tiny faces filled with cosmic wonder. Let their unbridled enthusiasm be contagious.

Think back to your own childhood. What were the things that sparked your curiosity and filled you with awe? Was it the feeling of sand warm between your toes on a sandy beach, the sound of rain drumming a rhythmic melody against the windowpane, or the sight of fireflies twinkling like stars in the summer night? Reconnecting with these childhood memories can help you tap into your own sense of wonder and appreciate the world through a fresh lens.

Now, imagine experiencing those same sensations through your child's eyes. See the world as a kaleidoscope of colors, sounds, and textures, where every puddle transforms into a potential splash zone, every tree a towering fortress to be conquered, and every raindrop a precious jewel glistening in the sunlight. By allowing yourself to be swept away by your child's enthusiasm and curiosity, you'll not only deepen your connection with them but also reawaken your own sense of wonder. You'll start to notice the intricate patterns on a butterfly's wings, the way sunlight filters through the leaves of a towering oak, and the symphony of sounds that fills a bustling park.

This shift in perspective can be transformative. It can help you break free from the monotony of routine, find joy in unexpected places, and appreciate the beauty that surrounds you every day. When you see the world through your child's eyes, you'll find that the ordinary becomes extraordinary, and the mundane is filled with magic. The simple act of blowing bubbles can become a breathtaking display of iridescence, a walk in the park can turn into a treasure hunt for hidden wonders, and a bedtime story can transport you to far-off lands filled with dragons and fairies.

So, the next time your child stops to admire a dandelion or gets excited about a passing train, take a moment to join them in their awe. Let their curiosity be contagious, their enthusiasm infectious. Embrace the childlike wonder that still resides within you, and allow it to color your world with a kaleidoscope of joy. By rediscovering the world through your child's eyes, you'll not only enrich your own life but also create lasting memories and deepen your bond with your child.

In the next section, we'll explore the power of vulnerability in parenting and how embracing the phrase "I don't know" can actually strengthen your connection with your child and create a more authentic learning environment for both of you.

In Action: Rediscovering Wonder

✓ **The Nature Walk Revelation:** John, a busy professional accustomed to a fast-paced life, found his patience wearing thin during weekend nature walks with his daughter, Lily. He viewed them as a chore, a distraction from his ever-growing to-do list. However, one day, as Lily excitedly pointed out a family of deer grazing in the distance, John decided to truly be present in the moment. He knelt down to Lily's level, examined the deer with genuine curiosity, and listened intently as she peppered him with questions about their behavior. This shared experience sparked a sense of wonder in John, reminding him of the simple joys of connecting with nature.

✓ **The Cardboard Box Castle:** Monica, a highly organized mom, struggled with her son Ethan's messy and imaginative play. His constant requests to transform the living room furniture into elaborate forts left her feeling frustrated and overwhelmed. One rainy afternoon, however, Monica decided to embrace Ethan's imaginative world. Together, they transformed a cardboard box into a magnificent castle, complete with towers and drawbridges. This experience allowed Monica to reconnect with her own childhood sense of wonder and appreciate the power of imaginative play.

The Power of "I Don't Know": Vulnerability as a Strength in the Parenting Journey

Have you ever been stumped by a question from your five-year-old? "Why is the sky blue?" they ask, their eyes wide with an insatiable curiosity that seems to hold the weight of the universe. The pressure to have all the answers can be overwhelming, a constant urge to uphold the illusion of parental omniscience. We scramble for explanations, fearing the disappointment that might flicker in their innocent eyes if we confess our limitations. But what if the most powerful tool in your parenting arsenal isn't some grand explanation, but two simple words: "I don't know."

Saying "I don't know" isn't a weakness, it's a liberation. It sheds the burden of the "perfect parent" myth and replaces it with something far more valuable: authenticity. It shows your child that you're human, that you're on a journey of learning alongside them, a fellow explorer in the vast unknown. Imagine the scenario: your child points to a streak of fluffy white clouds drifting across the endless expanse of blue and asks, "Why is the sky blue?" Instead of fumbling for a potentially confusing explanation about wavelengths and scattering light, you can respond with a genuine, "Wow, that's a great question! I don't know, but let's find out together!"

Suddenly, you're not just a dispenser of information, but a fellow explorer embarking on a shared adventure. The library becomes your launchpad, books your rocketship fuel. Together, you delve into the wonders of science, uncovering the fascinating reasons behind the sky's beautiful hue. The quest for knowledge becomes a bonding experience, fostering curiosity, critical thinking, and a sense of shared accomplishment in your child.

More importantly, by modeling vulnerability, you give your child permission to embrace their own uncertainties. You show them that it's okay to make mistakes, that asking for help is a sign of strength, not weakness, and that learning is a continuous journey, not a destination. Your child feels comfortable sharing their struggles and seeking your guidance, knowing that you're not just a source of answers, but a partner in exploration.

"I don't know" isn't just about knowledge; it's about connection. It builds a relationship based on mutual respect, trust, and a shared sense of wonder. You show your child that even grown-ups have things to learn, and that discovery is a lifelong adventure, best enjoyed together. It's about creating a space where wonder flourishes, where questions are celebrated, and where the journey of learning is as important as the destination.

This shift towards shared exploration goes beyond intellectual curiosity. It cultivates a deeper connection built on trust, authenticity, and a love of learning. When we embrace vulnerability and let go of the need to have all the answers, we open the door to a more meaningful and fulfilling parenting experience. In the next chapter, we'll explore the profound transformation of parenthood, the shift from "me" to "we," and how building a family-centered life can bring a sense of joy, purpose, and belonging that enriches us all.

In Action: The Power of "I Don't Know" 

✓ The Constellation Caper: Mark, a single father juggling multiple jobs, often felt overwhelmed by his son's boundless curiosity. Bedtime stories were a source of stress, as he worried he wouldn't have all the answers to Leo's questions about the twinkling stars above. One night, Mark decided to be honest about his limitations. He admitted he didn't know all the constellations but suggested they explore them together. Using a star chart and their imaginations, they embarked on a journey through the cosmos, creating their own fantastical stories about the constellations. This experience highlighted the importance of shared exploration and the power of vulnerability in building a strong parent-child bond.

Make it Happen: Turning Questions into Journeys 

✓ Level Up Your Parenthood:
  • Embrace the Wonder of "I Don't Know": Reframe "I

don't know" as a springboard for discovery. Use it as an opportunity to explore and learn with your child.

- **Turn Questions into Adventures:** Transform your child's questions into exciting quests for knowledge. Visit the library, conduct experiments, or explore online resources together.
- **Model Vulnerability:** Be open about your own uncertainties and mistakes. Show your child that it's okay not to have all the answers.
- **Celebrate the Journey of Learning:** Focus on the discovery process, not just the answer itself. Applaud your child's curiosity and encourage them to ask questions.
- **Create a Safe Space for Exploration:** Foster an environment where your child feels comfortable asking questions without fear of judgment.

From Me to We: *Shifting Priorities and Building a Family-Centered Life*

Ah, those carefree days of late-night adventures and leisurely brunches – a cherished memory perhaps, but parenthood doesn't have to signal the end of fun. Instead, it's an invitation to a new kind of joy, woven from connection, shared experiences, and a deeper sense of purpose.

Think of it as a beautiful shift in focus, from "me" to "we." Parenthood ushers in a reordering of priorities, where your family's needs bloom front and center. But this doesn't mean neglecting yourself. It's about finding a new balance and integrating your dreams and aspirations into the vibrant tapestry of family life.

Your definition of "fun" might evolve. Solo adventures transform into exploring nature trails with a giggling toddler in tow. Personal projects give way to the messy joy of family game nights. Career achievements are replaced by the immense satisfaction of nurturing your child's growth. Parenthood can be a surprising wellspring of personal growth, revealing hidden talents and passions you never knew you possessed. You might discover a knack for crafting fantastical Halloween costumes or rediscover your love of music through lullabies sung at bedtime.

Imagine family meals – a distraction-free haven for conversation, connection, and shared experiences. Turn off the screens and make mealtimes a sacred space for family bonding. Create special bedtime routines that promote closeness, like reading stories, singing lullabies, or simply cuddling. These cherished traditions become lasting memories. Dedicate weekends to family adventures, whether it's park trips, movie nights, or volunteering together. These shared experiences create the threads that bind your family closer. Get creative! Exploring new hobbies together – hiking, kayaking, or museum visits can spark unexpected passions.

Building a family-centered life is an ongoing journey, demanding patience, flexibility, and the willingness to adapt as your family grows and changes. It won't always be easy, but the rewards are immeasurable. By prioritizing your family and creating a loving, laughter-filled home, you nurture your children and cultivate a deep sense of joy and fulfillment in your own life.

Remember, self-care isn't selfish; it's essential. Recharge with activities that rejuvenate you – exercise, hobbies, or even some quiet time alone. A well-rested you is a better parent. Don't hesitate to ask for help from your partner, family, friends, or a therapist. Parenting is a team effort, and it takes a village. Embrace the journey. Parenthood is a constant adventure, full of unexpected twists. There will be spilled milk and sleepless nights, but also moments of pure joy – the first giggle, the wobbly first steps, the whispered "I love you" at bedtime. Savor these precious moments, big and small. Learn to find humor in the chaos, celebrate the victories (no matter how small), and weather the challenges with grace. Remember, the journey itself, with all its messiness and wonder, is just as important as the destination.

As you embrace this shift from "me" to "we," you might be surprised to discover hidden talents and abilities. Parenthood can be a boot camp for personal growth, pushing you outside your comfort zone and unlocking reserves of strength you never knew you possessed. In the next section, we'll delve into these unexpected superpowers, revealing the "Unexpected Superhero" within you.

In Action: The "We" Approach 

✓ The Rekindled Musician: David, a former aspiring musician, put his musical dreams on hold after the birth of his son, Mark.

He felt guilty prioritizing his interests and convinced himself he no longer had time for music. However, his wife encouraged him to integrate his passion into their family life. David began incorporating musical elements into their playtime, singing silly songs and using pots and pans as drums. Mark's infectious enthusiasm rekindled David's love for music, and he eventually started a family band, performing silly songs for them during playtime.

The Unexpected Superhero: Uncovering Hidden Strengths You Never Knew You Had

Parenthood, it turns out, is a bit like Clark Kent stepping into a phone booth – minus the spandex and the dramatic reveal, of course. It has a way of transforming ordinary individuals into unexpected superheroes, revealing hidden strengths and talents that were lying dormant, just waiting to be unleashed.

Perhaps you never thought of yourself as particularly patient, yet you find yourself calmly navigating toddler tantrums with the grace of a Zen master. Maybe you doubted your creativity, but now you're a pro at inventing silly songs and imaginative bedtime stories. Or perhaps you thought you were a mediocre cook, but suddenly you're whipping up nutritious meals that your picky eater actually devours.

The truth is, parenthood is a crash course in personal development. It pushes us to expand our skillset, adapt to new challenges, and discover hidden reservoirs of strength and resilience. We become masters of multitasking, experts in conflict resolution, and creative problem-solvers who can MacGyver a diaper out of a sock and a scarf in a pinch.

Think of all the times you've surprised yourself with your ability to stay calm under pressure, your knack for diffusing meltdowns, or your resourcefulness in finding solutions to unexpected problems. These are not just parenting skills; they are life skills that can serve you well in all areas of your life. Whether it's negotiating a raise at work, mediating a conflict between friends, or simply finding a creative solution to a household dilemma, the skills you've honed as a parent can translate into success in other areas of your life.

Parenthood also has a way of revealing our hidden talents. Maybe you discover a knack for photography as you capture your child's milestones, or perhaps you unleash your inner artist as you create homemade birthday cakes and decorations. Or maybe you find that you have a gift for teaching as you patiently explain complex concepts to your curious little one. These newfound talents can open up exciting possibilities for personal expression and growth.

Don't be afraid to explore them and see where they lead you! Perhaps your newfound photography skills inspire you to start a side business, or maybe your love of teaching leads you to volunteer at a local school. Your child isn't the only one who's growing and learning – parenthood is an opportunity for your evolution as well.

As you embrace the challenges and joys of parenthood, be open to the unexpected ways it can transform you. Celebrate your newfound skills and talents, and don't be afraid to step outside your comfort zone. You might just discover that you're capable of more than you ever imagined. After all, every superhero has an origin story, and yours might just be unfolding right before your eyes.

This journey of self-discovery isn't just about you; it also sets a powerful example for your child. By embracing your growth and showing them that it's okay to try new things, make mistakes, and learn along the way, you're teaching them invaluable life lessons about resilience, adaptability, and the importance of pursuing their passions.

As you grow as a parent, you'll inspire your child to do the same. They'll see that it's okay to be imperfect, that challenges can be overcome, and that lifelong learning is a journey, not a destination.

Parenting isn't a solo mission. It's a team effort, a symphony of support, guidance, and love. Just as you're discovering your own hidden strengths, you can also tap into the unique skills and expertise of others who share in your child's journey. While discovering and embracing your strengths as a parent is crucial, it's equally important to recognize that you don't have to go it alone. Your child's journey is enriched by a whole community of caring individuals who can offer unique perspectives, skills, and support.

In the next part, we'll delve into the importance of fostering strong relationships with the people who play a pivotal role in your child's life. We'll explore how to collaborate effectively with teachers, daycare providers, doctors, therapists, and other professionals who can provide valuable guidance and expertise. Just as a village raises a child, a network of caring adults can help your child thrive, learn, and grow. By building strong partnerships with these individuals, you're not just strengthening your support system; you're also creating a nurturing environment where your child can reach their full potential.

Mindful Parenting: Your Ideal Parenting Power 

✓ Pause & Reflect:
- What are some of the challenges you've faced as a parent?
- Imagine your ideal parent superhero power. What would it be?
- What are you grateful for about your personal growth as a parent?

"

"The more that you trust and empower your children, the more they will rise to meet your expectations."

- EMILIE BARNES
(An American positive psychology coach)

Part 8:

Building Your Child's Village: Caregivers, Educators, and Healthcare Professionals

Inside This Part

Parenting is a journey that's rarely taken alone. In fact, it often takes a village to raise a child, a supportive network of individuals who share in the joys and challenges of nurturing young minds. Think of it as a team effort, with each member playing a unique and valuable role in your child's development.

In this part, we'll explore how to build and nurture your child's village. We'll delve into the importance of collaborating with caregivers, educators, and healthcare professionals, forming trusting partnerships that empower your child to thrive. From effective communication strategies to understanding each team member's unique contributions, you'll gain the knowledge and skills you need to create a supportive and enriching environment for your child's growth.

We'll also explore how to advocate for your child's needs, ensuring they receive the best possible care and support at every stage of their development. This part is your guide to building a strong and collaborative team that will help your child reach their full potential, both inside and outside of the home.

Effective Communication and Collaboration: *Building Trusting Partnerships with Your Child's Team*

Think of your child's journey as an epic adventure, filled with exciting discoveries, challenges to overcome, and milestones to celebrate. You, as their parents, are their trusty guide, but you're not alone on this quest. Surrounding your child is a team of experienced adventurers – caregivers, educators, and healthcare professionals – each with their unique skills and knowledge to share. They may be teachers who ignite a love of learning, caregivers who provide nurturing support, or doctors who ensure their physical well-being. Together, you form a powerful alliance, dedicated to helping your child thrive.

Like any successful team, the key to navigating this journey is effective communication and collaboration. Imagine a group of explorers huddled around a map, sharing their insights, strategies, and concerns. In the same way, open and honest communication with your child's "team" can create a shared vision for their well-being and foster a collaborative approach to their care.

This starts with building trusting partnerships. Think of these relationships as bridges, connecting you with the people who play a vital role in your child's life. These bridges are built on mutual respect, open communication, and a shared commitment to your child's best interests.

Take the time to get to know the people who care and educate your child. Attend school events, schedule meetings with teachers and caregivers, and ask questions about their approach to child development. Share information about your child's strengths, challenges, and any concerns you may have. The more you understand each other's perspectives and goals, the stronger your partnership will become. These professionals have a wealth of experience and knowledge to share, and they can offer valuable insights that you might not have considered.

Open and honest communication is the cornerstone of any successful team. Here are some tips for fostering effective communication with your child's team:

- **Be proactive:** Initiate conversations and reach out regularly, not just when problems arise. Regular check-ins, whether through emails, phone calls, or in-person meetings, can help you stay informed about your child's progress and address any concerns early on.
- **Listen actively:** Give your full attention when others are speaking, and reflect back on what you hear to ensure understanding. This shows that you value their input and are committed to working together.

- **Share information openly:** Be transparent about your child's needs, challenges, and successes. This helps create a comprehensive picture of your child and enables your team to tailor their support accordingly.
- **Ask questions:** Don't be afraid to ask for clarification, seek advice, or express concerns. No question is too small or insignificant when it comes to your child's well-being.
- **Be respectful:** Even when you disagree, maintain a respectful and collaborative tone. Remember that everyone on your child's team has the same goal: to help your child thrive.

You are the expert on your child. Don't be afraid to advocate for their needs, share your insights, and ask questions. By working together with your child's team, you can create a holistic and supportive environment that nurtures their development in all areas of life. This collaborative approach not only benefits your child but also empowers you as a parent, providing you with a wealth of knowledge and resources to draw upon as you guide your child on their exciting journey of growth and discovery.

Beyond formal meetings and communication, there are other ways to foster connections with your child's team:

- **Show appreciation:** A simple thank-you note or a small gift can go a long way in showing your gratitude for their dedication and support.
- **Offer help:** Volunteer your time or expertise to help out in the classroom or at your child's daycare.
- **Create a sense of community:** Organize social events or gatherings where parents, teachers, and caregivers can connect and build relationships.

Building a strong team takes time and effort. Invest in these relationships, and you'll reap the rewards of a supportive network that's committed to your child's well-being. Don't be afraid to seek help. Your child's team is there to support you, so don't hesitate to reach out when you need guidance or advice. Celebrate the victories together. When your child achieves a milestone or overcomes a challenge, acknowledge the contributions of their entire team. This reinforces the power of collaboration and creates a sense of shared pride and accomplishment.

By working together, you and your child's team can create a powerful force for good, guiding your child towards a bright and fulfilling future. In the next section, we'll delve deeper into the specific roles and responsibilities of each member of your child's team, providing you with practical tips for building strong partnerships that will benefit your child for years to come.

Make it Happen: Building Strong Partnerships 

- ✓ Level Up Your Parenthood:
  - **Stay in the Loop:** Schedule regular check-ins with your child's teacher, daycare provider, or doctor. These conversations allow you to stay informed about your child's progress, address any concerns, and work collaboratively with their support system.
  - **Be a Partner in Learning:** Collaborate with your child's educators to understand their curriculum and learning goals for your child.
  - **Empower Your Child:** Help your child learn to advocate for themselves, encouraging them to communicate their needs effectively.

- **Become an Advocate:** Advocate for your child's needs and ask questions if you have any concerns. Don't hesitate to speak up if you feel your child requires additional support or has specific needs that aren't being met.
- **Expand Your Network:** Join a parent-teacher association (PTA) or similar organization to connect with other parents and educators. This allows you to share information, find support, and gain valuable insights from other parents and professionals in your child's school community.

Working Together:
Building Strong Partnerships with Your Child's Team

Consider this: you and your child's team are like a crew of skilled mountaineers, each with a unique set of skills and expertise, working together to summit the peak of your child's potential. You, the parent, are the base camp, providing the foundation and emotional support. Your child's teachers, caregivers, and healthcare professionals are the sherpas, guiding them through the challenging terrain of learning, social development, and physical well-being. Together, you form an unstoppable team, bound by a shared goal of helping your child reach new heights.

But like any climbing team, success depends on strong partnerships and clear communication. Imagine a team of climbers ascending a treacherous peak. They rely on each other's strengths, communicate openly about challenges, and celebrate victories together. Similarly, your child's team can achieve incredible things when you work together, share insights, and pool your resources.

So how do you build these strong partnerships? Start by recognizing that everyone on the team has a unique role. Teachers offer expertise in curriculum and learning styles, providing invaluable insights into your child's academic progress and potential areas for growth. Caregivers provide nurturing care and support outside of school, offering a safe and loving environment for your child to explore and develop their social-emotional skills. Healthcare professionals ensure your child's physical and mental health, monitoring their development and addressing any concerns that arise. By understanding each member's contribution, you can better appreciate the value they bring to your child's life.

Just as climbers adjust their strategies based on the terrain and weather conditions, your child's team may need to adapt their approach as your child grows and changes. Regular check-ins, open communication, and a willingness to collaborate can help you navigate these changes together.

These check-ins can take many forms:

- **Formal meetings:** Schedule regular parent-teacher conferences, meet with your child's therapist, or have discussions with your pediatrician to discuss progress and concerns. These meetings provide a structured setting to share information, set goals, and develop strategies for supporting your child. Come prepared with questions and observations, and be open to hearing feedback from the professionals.

- **Informal conversations:** Chat with your child's teacher after school, exchange emails with their caregiver, or have a quick phone call with their doctor to clarify any questions. These informal interactions can build rapport and foster a sense of trust. They can also be a quick and easy way to address minor concerns or share positive feedback.

- **Written communication:** Use a notebook or online platform to share observations and information between home and school/daycare. This can be a valuable tool for tracking your child's progress, sharing strategies that work at home, and ensuring everyone is on the same page.

Your child's team is your ally, not your adversary. Approach these relationships with trust, respect, and a willingness to learn from each other. Together, you can create a harmonious and supportive environment where your child can thrive and reach their full potential. By fostering a strong sense of teamwork and collaboration, you're not only benefiting your child in the present but also equipping them with valuable skills for navigating relationships and achieving success in the future.

The journey of parenting and child development is not always smooth sailing. There will be challenges along the way, whether it's a learning difficulty, a behavioral issue, or a health concern. When faced with these challenges, it's crucial to lean on your child's team for support and guidance. They are experts in their respective fields, and their insights can be invaluable in helping you find solutions and strategies.

Maintain open communication with your child's team during these challenging times. Share your observations and concerns, ask for their advice, and be open to their suggestions. By working together, you can create a comprehensive and effective plan to address the issue and support your child's overall well-being.

The goal is to create a united front, where everyone is working together to support your child's growth and well-being. By fostering strong partnerships and open communication, you can create a harmonious and empowering environment where your child can thrive.

In the next section, we'll delve deeper into the individual roles that each member of your child's team plays. We'll explore the unique expertise and contributions of caregivers, educators, and healthcare professionals, so you can better understand how to collaborate with them effectively and advocate for your child's needs.

In Action: Building Strong Partnerships

- ✓ **The United Front:** Emily, a single mom, felt overwhelmed by her son Ethan's sudden struggles in school. She noticed a decline in his grades and a withdrawal from social interaction. However, through open communication with Ethan's teacher, Ms. Jones, Emily discovered that Ethan was experiencing anxiety related to an upcoming standardized test. Ms. Jones shared calming strategies used in the classroom, and Emily implemented similar techniques at home. Together, they formed a united front, providing Ethan consistent support and reassurance. Ethan's anxiety subsided, his grades improved, and he reconnected with his classmates.

✓ The Listening Therapist: David and Maria felt unheard when it came to their daughter Lily's speech development. Their pediatrician dismissed their concerns, but they persisted, reaching out to a speech therapist recommended by a friend. The therapist, Ms. Garcia, actively listened to their observations and conducted a thorough evaluation. She then developed a personalized therapy plan and provided David and Maria with strategies to support Lily's communication at home. Through open collaboration and ongoing communication, Lily's speech skills blossomed, and her parents felt empowered advocates for her development.

Knowing Your Team: *Understanding Each Member's Contribution*

Imagine a symphony orchestra, each musician playing a different instrument, each contributing their unique sound to create a harmonious melody. Your child's "village" is much like this orchestra, with each member playing a vital role in their development. The ensemble of individuals who support, guide, and nurture them directly impacts the richness and depth of your child's life.

Let's take a closer look at the key players in your child's symphony of support:

- **The Conductor:** As the parent, you are the conductor of this orchestra. You set the tone, establish the rhythm, and guide the overall direction of your child's development. You provide the emotional foundation, the safe haven, and the unconditional love that allows your child to flourish. Just as a conductor interprets a musical score, you interpret your child's needs and cues, adapting your approach to ensure their well-being and growth. Your love and guidance are the melodies that bind the entire orchestra together.

- **The String Section:** Caregivers, whether they are nannies, babysitters, or family members, provide the gentle, nurturing melodies that soothe and comfort your child. They offer a consistent presence, build trust, and create a sense of security that allows your child to explore the world with confidence. Like the soothing strings of a violin, caregivers offer warmth and reassurance, creating a harmonious backdrop for your child's development.

- **The Brass Section:** Educators, such as teachers and tutors, are the bold, vibrant voices that ignite your child's curiosity and inspire a love of learning. They introduce new ideas, challenge assumptions, and provide the tools for your child to reach their full academic potential. Like the powerful sound of a trumpet, educators awaken the mind and inspire children to explore new horizons.

- **The Woodwind Section:** Healthcare professionals, including pediatricians, therapists, and specialists, are the steady, reassuring voices that ensure your child's physical and mental well-being. They monitor your child's growth, diagnose and treat illnesses, and provide guidance on healthy habits. Just as the gentle tones of a flute can soothe a troubled heart, healthcare professionals offer support and expertise to ensure your child thrives physically and emotionally.
- **The Percussion Section:** The broader community, including coaches, mentors, religious leaders, and neighbors, add depth and richness to your child's symphony of support. They offer unique perspectives, experiences, and opportunities for growth, helping your child develop a sense of belonging and connection to the world around them. Like the rhythmic beat of a drum, the community provides a steady pulse that anchors your child to their roots and propels them forward.

By understanding the unique role each member plays in your child's life, you can better appreciate their contributions and collaborate effectively to create a harmonious and supportive environment for your child's growth. Each instrument in an orchestra is important, and when they play together in sync, they create a masterpiece. Similarly, each member of your child's village plays a crucial part in their development, and by fostering collaboration and communication, you can create a harmonious symphony of support that nurtures their bright mind and helps them reach their full potential.

Just as each instrument in the orchestra has a specific part to play, each member of your child's team brings unique expertise and perspective to the table. By understanding their roles and collaborating effectively, you can create a harmonious symphony of support that nurtures your child's growth and development.

But what happens when the music falters, when your child's needs aren't being met, or when you disagree with the approach of a team member? In the next section, we'll explore the importance of advocating for your child, finding your voice as a parent, and ensuring that your child's unique needs are heard and addressed within the context of this collaborative team.

In Action: Recognizing Expertise

✓ **The Unexpected Therapist:** John and Mary worried about their daughter Emily's social anxiety. While their pediatrician offered general advice, they felt a more targeted approach was needed. Remembering their neighbor, Sarah, who worked as a therapist specializing in childhood anxiety, they reached out for guidance. Sarah, understanding the complexities of social anxiety in children, provided John and Mary with practical strategies and connected them with additional resources. By recognizing Sarah's expertise and collaborating with her, John and Mary felt empowered to help Emily overcome her anxiety and build stronger social connections.

Empowering Yourself:
Advocating for Your Child's Needs

Picture this: You're sitting in a meeting with your child's teacher, and a wave of unease washes over you. The teacher is describing behaviors you've never witnessed at home, and their suggested approach doesn't feel quite right for your child. Your heart pounds, your palms sweat, and your mind races with doubts. Should you speak up? Challenge their assessment? Or simply nod and smile, trusting the "expert's" opinion?

This scenario is familiar to many parents. The desire to advocate for our children is fierce, but so too is the fear of overstepping, of not being taken seriously, or of making things worse. But remember, you are your child's first and foremost advocate. You know them better than anyone and your instincts are powerful tools for navigating this complex terrain.

Advocating for your child doesn't mean being confrontational or combative. It's about finding your voice, expressing your concerns with respect and clarity, and working collaboratively with your child's team to find solutions that benefit everyone. Here are some strategies for empowering yourself as an advocate:

- **Trust Your Gut:** If something doesn't feel right, don't ignore it. Your instincts are often a reliable guide, rooted in your deep knowledge of your child. You've spent countless hours with your child, observing their quirks, their strengths, and their challenges. Trust that inner voice that tells you when something isn't quite right.

- **Prepare for Conversations:** Before meeting with your child's team, take some time to reflect on your concerns and observations. Write down specific questions or points you want to discuss. This preparation can help you stay focused and articulate your thoughts clearly. You have the right to ask for clarification, request additional information, or seek a second opinion.

- **Speak Up Respectfully:** Express your concerns clearly and directly, using "I" statements to avoid blame or accusation. For example, instead of saying, "You're wrong about my child," try saying, "I'm concerned about this approach because..." Framing your concerns this way can help open dialogue and avoid defensiveness.

- **Seek Collaboration:** You and your child's team are working towards a common goal – your child's well-being. Focus on finding solutions that benefit everyone, rather than getting caught up in power struggles or disagreements. Be open to hearing different perspectives, ask questions, and be willing to compromise.

- **Know Your Rights:** Familiarize yourself with your child's rights in educational and healthcare settings. This knowledge can empower you to advocate effectively and ensure your child receives the support they need. Understand the laws and regulations that protect your child's rights, and don't hesitate to seek legal advice if necessary.

- **Seek Support:** If you feel overwhelmed or uncertain, don't hesitate to seek support from other parents, advocacy groups, or legal professionals. You're not alone in this journey. Connecting with other parents who have faced similar challenges can provide valuable insights and encouragement.

You are your child's most powerful advocate. By embracing your role, trusting your instincts, and communicating effectively, you can ensure that their unique needs are met and that they receive the support they deserve.

Advocating for your child is not about being a perfect parent; it's about being a present and engaged one. It's about trusting your instincts, using your voice, and working collaboratively with your child's team to create the best possible outcome for your child. It's about being your child's champion, ensuring their voice is heard and their needs are met. And in doing so, you'll not only empower your child but also strengthen your own confidence and resilience as a parent.

As you embrace your role as an advocate, remember that your voice matters. By speaking up for your child's needs, you're not only empowering them to thrive but also honoring the unique bond you share. And as you build a strong and supportive village around your child, you're laying the foundation for a lifetime of growth, learning, and connection.

In the final chapter of this book, we'll come full circle, revisiting the enduring power of connection and reflecting on the incredible journey of parenthood. We'll celebrate the milestones, acknowledge the challenges, and embrace the beautiful messiness that makes this adventure so rewarding. Let's dive in and explore the lasting impact of the connection you've built with your child.

✓ **The Questioning Parent:** John wasn't convinced that the standardized testing approach favored his son, Ethan, who thrived in a more hands-on learning environment. Despite initial hesitation, John decided to meet Ethan's teacher, Mr. Davis. John expressed his concerns respectfully, highlighting Ethan's strengths and learning style. Mr. Davis appreciated John's insights and offered alternative assessment methods that better suited Ethan's needs. John' advocacy ensured that Ethan's unique learning style was valued and nurtured within the classroom.

66

"The most important thing that parents can teach their children is how to get along without them."

- ROBERT FROST
(An American poet)

Conclusion:

The Journey of Parenthood: Building a Foundation for a Lifetime

Inside This Part

As we reach the final pages of this journey together, let's take a moment to reflect on the incredible adventure you've embarked upon as a parent. We've explored the wonders of child development, the power of connection, the importance of setting boundaries, and the unexpected ways in which parenting can shape and transform us.

But parenting isn't just about knowledge and skills; it's about relationships, growth, and the enduring power of love. In conclusion, we'll celebrate the milestones you've achieved, acknowledge the challenges you've faced, and look ahead to the future with hope and optimism.

We'll also explore how gentle parenting is not a destination, but an ongoing process of learning, adapting, and deepening your connection with your child. It's about embracing the ups and downs, celebrating the joys, and learning from the missteps along the way. Most importantly, it's about creating a loving and supportive environment where your child can thrive and become the best version of themselves.

The Enduring Power of Connection: Building a Foundation for a Lifetime

It's important to remember that the true magic lies in the connections we forge with our children. These connections are not simply a means to an end, but a source of deep joy, resilience, and growth for both parent and child.

Think of it like a sturdy tree, its roots reaching deep into the earth, providing nourishment and stability. The connection you build with your child is that root system, grounding them in love, security, and understanding. It's a bond that can weather any storm, a foundation that supports them as they grow and blossom into their full potential.

This connection is not built overnight. It's a continuous process, nurtured through countless moments of shared laughter, quiet conversations, comforting hugs, and shared experiences. It's the bedtime stories whispered in the dark, the silly dances in the kitchen, the heart-to-heart talks on long car rides, and the silent comfort of simply being present.

The enduring power of connection lies in its ability to transcend time and distance. It's the feeling of warmth that spreads through your chest when your child reaches out for a hug, the pride that swells in your heart as you watch them achieve a milestone, and the deep sense of knowing that you are loved and cherished, even when mistakes are made.

This connection is not just about the good times; it's also about weathering the storms together. It's about offering a safe haven when your child is struggling, a listening ear when they need to vent, and gentle guidance when they've lost their way. It's about showing up, even when it's hard, and reminding your child that they are never alone.

As your child grows and changes, so will your relationship. The connection you've built will evolve, deepen, and take on new dimensions. But the foundation you've laid – a foundation of love, trust, and understanding – will remain a constant source of strength and support for both of you.

This unbreakable bond, woven with threads of love, trust, and understanding, is the most precious gift you can give your child. It's a legacy that will last a lifetime, shaping their relationships, their self-worth, and their overall well-being.

As we conclude this guide to gentle parenting, let's take a moment to reflect on the incredible journey you've embarked upon. In the next section, we'll celebrate the milestones you and your child have achieved, the lessons you've learned, and the growth you've experienced together. We'll also look ahead to the future, armed with the tools and insights you need to continue fostering a strong and loving connection with your child for years to come.

Reflecting on Growth: *Celebrating Milestones and Your Personal Journey*

Take a moment to pause and look back at the path you've traveled as a parent. Think of all the milestones you and your child have celebrated together—the first smiles, the first steps, the first words, the first day of school. Remember the sleepless nights, the laughter-filled afternoons, the heart-to-heart talks, and the quiet moments of connection. Each of these moments has shaped you, challenged you, and ultimately, made you the parent you are today.

Parenting is a journey of constant growth both for you and your child. It's a beautiful dance of learning, adapting, and evolving together. As your child grows, so do you. You learn new skills, you develop new strengths, and you discover new depths of love and patience within yourself.

Reflect on the ways parenthood has changed you. Maybe you've become more patient, more empathetic, or more resilient. Perhaps you've discovered hidden talents, passions, or strengths you never knew you had. Or maybe you've simply gained a deeper appreciation for the simple joys of life, the beauty of a shared smile, or the warmth of a snuggle on the couch.

Take a moment to celebrate these milestones, big and small. Acknowledge the challenges you've overcome, the lessons you've learned, and the progress you've made. Parenting is not about perfection; it's about showing up every day, doing your best, and loving your child unconditionally.

As you look back on your journey, take pride in the parent you've become. You are a superhero in your own right, a guiding light for your child, a source of unwavering love and support. And as you continue on this path, remember that the journey is just as important as the destination. Embrace the ups and downs, the laughter and tears, the triumphs and setbacks. For it is in these moments that you'll find the true meaning of parenthood—the enduring power of connection, the joy of shared growth, and the unbreakable bond you've built with your child.

The path of parenthood is not always smooth, but the rewards are immeasurable. As we move into our final thoughts in this book, remember that even amidst the challenges and the messy, beautiful chaos, there's an undeniable truth: parenting is a journey of growth, not just for our children, but for ourselves. It's a dance of love, learning, and transformation.

In the next section, we'll embrace the full spectrum of this journey—the laughter and tears, the triumphs and setbacks. We'll explore how gentle parenting is a lifelong process of learning and growing alongside our children, and how embracing the ups and downs can lead to deeper connections, greater resilience, and a more joyful parenting experience.

Embrace the Ups and Downs:
Gentle Parenting is a Lifelong Process

As we reach the final pages of our parenting journey together, let's acknowledge a fundamental truth: parenting is not a destination, but an ever-evolving adventure. It's a winding road with unexpected detours, hairpin turns, and scenic overlooks. Some days you'll coast along smoothly, feeling confident and empowered. On other days, you'll encounter potholes and roadblocks, leaving you feeling frustrated and uncertain.

Gentle parenting is not a formula for perfection; it's a philosophy of growth, both for your child and for yourself. It's about embracing the entire spectrum of human experience, with all its messiness and beauty. It's about learning from your mistakes, celebrating your victories, and never giving up on the journey of connection.

Remember those moments of laughter and joy, the spontaneous hugs and whispered secrets, the shared adventures and quiet cuddles. These are the treasures you'll carry with you forever, the memories that will warm your heart and bring a smile to your face. But remember also the challenges, the sleepless nights, the tantrums, the teenage angst. These are not failures but rather opportunities for growth and deeper understanding.

Just as your child learns and grows through trial and error, so do you as a parent. Each challenge you face, each hurdle you overcome, strengthens your resilience, deepens your compassion, and expands your capacity for love. Embracing the ups and downs of parenting is not a sign of weakness but a testament to your strength and courage.

So, as you close this book, take a moment to acknowledge and celebrate your own journey as a parent. You are not perfect, but you are enough. You are a loving, caring, and capable guide for your child, and your commitment to gentle parenting is a gift that will continue to give for years to come. It is a lifelong journey, even when your child grows up and builds their own life. You will always be a parent as long as you are alive, and the bond you've created will continue to evolve and deepen over time.

As you continue on this extraordinary path, remember that gentle parenting is not just a set of techniques or strategies; it's a way of being, a philosophy that can enrich every aspect of your life. May your journey be filled with joy, laughter, and countless moments of connection. May you continue to grow alongside your child, discovering new depths of love, resilience, and compassion within yourself. And may you always remember the enduring power of connection, the foundation upon which bright minds are built and lifelong bonds are forged.

Acknowledgments

Building Bright Minds wouldn't have been possible without a village of support. My deepest gratitude goes to the countless parents who navigate the joys and challenges of raising children. Your stories and experiences fueled my desire to create this resource.

Special thanks to Dr. Amelia Wright, a leading expert in child development with a focus on early social-emotional learning. Her insights on fostering cooperation and communication skills in young children were invaluable. Your guidance helped shape this book into a practical and informative guide. To my editor, Mark Ellis, thank you for your keen eye and editorial magic. You transformed raw ideas into a clear and engaging resource for parents.

Finally, to my incredible family, especially Michael and Emily, your unwavering support and understanding were essential. You kept the spark alive during late nights and editing marathons.

And most importantly, to all parents raising curious, resilient, and confident children – this book is for you. May it empower you on your journey and provide tools for building a strong and loving bond with your little ones.

About The Author

For over a decade, I've seen the challenges parents face as a parenting coach. My own experiences, both as a therapist and a parent, fueled my desire to create a resource that empowers you to navigate every stage of your child's development. My approach is simple: bridge the gap between my professional training and my own experiences as a parent.

In "Building Bright Minds", I translate complex concepts into practical, down-to-earth guidance. This book equips you with the tools you need to build a strong bond with your child, navigate common challenges like tantrums and learning struggles, and foster emotional intelligence for a lifetime. Because let's face it, even the toughest moments can be opportunities for growth. With the right approach and consistent practice, we can help our children blossom into strong, confident, and resilient individuals.

When not writing or seeing clients, Sarah can be found hiking with her family, attempting to learn the piano, or experimenting with new vegetarian recipes.

Also by Sarah J. Foster:

Calming Social Anxiety for Teens: Simple CBT, ACT and Mindfulness practices to Boost Confidence, Overcome Fear, and Face Shyness in Groups

Does your teen struggle in social situations?

Feeling shy or anxious can be tough for teens. From the author of "Building Bright Minds," "Calming Social Anxiety for Teens" offers a practical guide packed with effective strategies to help them:

- Face social challenges with greater ease.
- Form stronger relationships with friends and family.
- Embrace opportunities and discover their full potential.

As a companion to "Building Bright Minds," "Calming Social Anxiety for Teens" empowers parents to nurture well-adjusted, confident children.